NOTES

FROM PLYMOUTH PULPIT.

NOTES

FROM

PLYMOUTH PULPIT:

A Collection of Memorable Passages

FROM THE

DISCOURSES OF HENRY WARD BEECHER,

BY AUGUSTA MOORE.

NEW YORK:
DERBY & JACKSON, 119 NASSAU STREET.
1859.

W. H. Tinson, Stereotyper.

Geo. Russell & Co., Printers.

PUBLISHERS' NOTICE.

THIS volume is published not only without preparation or revision by Mr. Beecher, but he is ignorant of its entire contents, he having seen neither the copy or the proof. In withdrawing his objections to the publication of it, Mr. Beecher was influenced by the same generous motives which prompted him to give to others than himself, the benefit of his previous published works. It is believed that the editor has faithfully caught the spirit of the living, breathing words, as uttered by the pastor of Plymouth Church; and that her work will be received with acceptance by the public.

INTRODUCTORY.

The Notes contained in this volume are chiefly from memory. The most of them were written during the years of 1856–7—and were committed to paper simply because it was impossible to think of, or to write, anything else with a mind so fully possessed by the memory of the sermons from which they were taken.

Mr. Beecher is not responsible for the contents of this volume. There is no pretension that the Notes are verbatim. Whether they are, in tone and spirit, *like him*, the public will judge. But, because a thing is written here, it must not be said to Mr. Beecher, "You said that thing," unless he chooses to own it. In repeating from memory the sayings of another, it is very likely that errors may occur. Meanings may be modified or colored by the mind through which they pass.

And yet the writer has tried faithfully to give the true sense, and, as far as memory would assist, the exact expressions of Mr. Beecher.

It is not the beauty of Mr. Beecher's expressions, nor

the startling and resplendent flashes of his thought that this book will show, so much as his presentation of simple and holy truth, in such guise as never fails to interest and instruct all whose notice is gained. And thousands who cannot be induced to peruse long sermons, will cheerfully read, and undoubtedly remember the vital truths illustrated and enforced in the following pages.

The volume is a testimony to the power with which the mind from whence it sprung influences other minds, and of the *nature* of that influence.

A. M.

CONTENTS.

A

B

C

D

HENRY WARD BEECHER.

When Henry Ward Beecher is dead, there will be made a great effort to learn just how he looked and acted, as well as just what he said.

And perhaps it will fall out, in his case, as it has in regard to many others of renown, that with much labor and with heavy cost, men shall succeed in discovering nothing very definite or reliable.

It is easy to enumerate the points in a man's personal appearance, if that were all. Mr. Beecher is of medium height, is full in flesh, has a strong, well developed frame; every organ is active and healthy. He has full command of his limbs, which are pliant and supple as a child's; his body is as elastic as an india-rubber ball, and handled by him with about as much ease as he would toss about a ball. His face is full and fresh; his eyes large, expressive, and blue—sometimes grey; his forehead is square and broad, his hair brown, and worn long; his glance quick, keen, and discerning; his smile humorous and pleasant.

Who, now, that has not seen the man, can tell how he appears to the eye that actually beholds him? and who can *ever* gather from such points the endless variety in a man's appearance?

To describe Mr. Beecher's mind, there are not half a dozen writers in the country who could be trusted ; and only the pen or the brush of a master could do anything like justice to his mere physical man. Would that there might arise, betimes, some efficient limner.

Like the mountains of which Mr. Beecher delights to talk, he has numberless diverse moods and aspects. Like them, he is sometimes cloudy and obscured ; and sometimes, like them, he stands out bold and clear, in the full light of noon.

Never was human face more variable ; of no one that ever lived could it more emphatically be said, "On different days he looks a different man."

At one time, and in one mood, his face is red, his eyes dull and half covered with the swollen flesh of the heavy lids. There is no brightness to be seen about him ; no briskness of motion, no erectness or strength of position. The animal nature has gained temporary ascendency over the spiritual, and an enemy might be *expected* to describe Mr. Beecher as an unrefined ploughboy, or a butcher in a minister's clothes, or rather, in a minister's desk, for Mr. Beecher's clothes are *not* ministerial.

But let the enemy wait until he sees our mountain in its more usual aspect. Let him wait until the strong, and perhaps somewhat rough and rugged intellect has stirred itself, and arisen for action, till the torpedo-like heart is on fire, till the fervid words burst forth, and the face, but now so dull, begins to shine with the interior glory.

Then comes the transfiguration! The material shrinks from sight, and the spiritual beams forth, causing in his countenance a change almost inconceivable. His face assumes all the rich softness of a mezzotint engraving—round, fair, and dimpled you *now* perceive it to be; and its whole expression becomes pure and elevated, almost like the angels' faces that we have seen in dreams.

His forehead is white and high, and shines like the brow of a sun-touched mountain; his eyes beam clear and mild, now with the strength of the man, again with love and innocence, like the eyes of a babe; his close-shaven chin, and the lower part of his cheeks are shaded, as if by the brush of an artist; there is no longer a rugged line, or a rough look about him, his aspect is *altogether* noble, beautiful, serene.

This, until he stands forth as Boanerges, and then he is the mountain in a winter storm. Mingling in his tones, are heard reminders of the cataract, and of the crash of thunder; while his flashing eyes and changing features have upon you the effect of lightning, and his gestures represent the rushing wind. Then, while you are yet thrilling to the sweep of the storm, you are melted to tears by some sorrow, or some longing, started into new life by the magic tenderness of tones silvery sweet.

Mr. Beecher's voice alone is a wonderful power. It mingles in its various utterances, all loud, and wild, and awful tones, with the sound of fairy harpstrings, and the chime of bells. It has the high battle-call of the trumpet or the clarion, and all the touching gentleness of a mother's cradle hymn.

A man whose voice combines the three sorts of power with which the three following sentences were spoken, has in his possession an engine fitted to move the world :

"When they come forth from their graves—when from mountain, from valley, and from the dark waves of the sea, they lift up their blanched faces to their Judge they will be speechless."

"Butterflies, the interior spirit of rainbows, sent down to salute those kisses of the seasons on the ground-flowers."

"Women, who have such need of love, *ought not* to find it hard to come to Jesus Christ, and put their arms about his neck, and tell him, with gushing love, that they give themselves, body and soul, into his keeping."

What has been said and written of Dr. Chalmers' pulpit appearance, manners, and diction, reminds one very forcibly of Mr. Beecher. As plain "in dress and gait" as was that celebrated preacher, and as impressive in discourse as he, is the subject of this sketch. Alike in plainness of speech, in intense earnestness, in quick and deep emotion, in apt and striking imagery and illustration, are the sermons of these two men—*Men.* Alike, in the sermons of each, when at full flood, deep calls unto deep, spirit speaks to spirit, and the hearer almost forgets that he yet wears the veil, and dwells amid the false and deceptive scenes of the flesh. Often it seems as if the judgment were already set, and the hearer there. Few, indeed, are the preachers who have power to strike directly to the heart, to lay hold with such forcible and tenacious grasp upon the moral sense, as does Henry Ward Beecher. Every man's soul may be reached in some way, and Mr. Beecher knows the open path. Let that man who does not wish his conscience roused, his nerves thrilled, and his tears started, keep away from the genuine and impassioned power of truth, as presented—as thrust in upon men's souls, by Henry Ward Beecher.

A cold, polished, cynical man of the world, going one evening, at the invitation of a lady, to Plymouth Church, remarked upon his way, "I go to hear Henry Ward Beecher with the same feelings that I go to witness the performances of Burton."

The sermon that night, though not one of Mr. Beecher's greatest efforts, was a powerful one, appealing to man's own consciousness of sin and ill desert ; every word told. There was no escape. It was extempore, only the heads thoroughly analyzed and accurately worded, being written out. The speaker's logic, at which the visitor had seemed inclined to sneer, was perfect ; and his presentation of the truth was truly appalling to all out of Christ.

The face of the gentleman who thought he was going to be amused that evening, belied his feelings if he *was* amused.

The aptness of Mr. Beecher's comparisons ; the acuteness with which he lays the knife to what *needs* cutting ; the unexpected descents which he makes upon errors of thought and conduct, frequently excite irresistible laughter. From this fact, those that lie in wait seeking how they may harm him, have represented him in the light of a clerical buffoon. Nothing can be more entirely or malignantly false. He is as far from levity and irreverence as those who purposely malign him are from nobleness and honesty. Gravity sits upon him with a native grace.

But his imagination is so rich and strong, his flow of language is so great, and the heart that beats like a great hammer in his breast, is such a volcanic heart, so impetuous, so prone to overflow, that he does sometimes lose the reins of prudence. He is occasionally like a man who has struck his foot so hard against a stone, that, to save himself from falling on his face, he needs *must* run awhile, though every step be upon vipers. The temperament which God gave a man must be considered in judging of him ; and considering that of Mr. Beecher, also the multitude of things that he has said, and is forever saying ; and the pressure of the various extreme excitements which are upon him ; it is a proof that he possesses a remarkable share of discretion and common sense that he has said *so few* imprudent things as he has said.

Mr. Beecher is frequently humorous, both in tone and expression, when he is altogether unaware that he is so. It is conceded that, great as is this orator, and nobly as truth and earnestness are stamped on all that he says and does, that master as he is of gesture and expression, there still is hovering about him somewhat of the ludicrous.

Certain notions he has which always incline one to

smile. The wag of his head when he is about to clinch an argument; the shake of his elbows and his knees, when he knows that he has you penned; the eagerness with which he seizes upon that devoted handkerchief, when he is about to "charge;" the strength with which, as he commences his tilt, he squeezes it (turning his hand-palm towards his chair and back towards the desk, leaning on knuckles and thumb, one foot crossed over the other, and supported upon its toe); the force with which he throws it from him, as he comes forward to close in the conflict he has waged; are all manœuvres certain to be repeated, almost constantly; and one cannot avoid being amused by seeing them so unconsciously, yet energetically, performed.

Although Mr. Beecher himself seldom appears to be in much haste, there is always an air of being in a hurry about his clothes and his hair. *They* manifest intentions of going forward, whether *he* goes or remains standing still. His neck is so short that he never ventures a standing-up collar. This, probably, in consideration for his ears.

One very remarkable singularity in his face is the utter incongruity between its front and its side views. Upon being told that he resembled Henry Ward Beecher, a relative of that clergyman replied, laughingly, "I know that I am said to look like him; but 'tis such resemblance as a sheep bears to a lion." Now the fact is, were that humble-minded relative of the famed "Lion" a great deal more like a "sheep" than he considers himself to be, he might *still* bear striking resemblance to his cousin; for though when he turns full towards you, in the heat of discourse, Mr. Beecher frequently does present the appearance of a lion, it is next to impossible for a person of an imaginative turn of mind to view his *profile* without being strongly reminded of ovine faces, seen and perhaps loved, in the days and the years gone by.

The timidity of the sheep is not there; but its long favoredness, its serenity, its gentleness, and modesty of expression, most certainly are. His face is mobile to the last degree: to the play of his features there appears to be no limit. There is not a feeling of the heart that he cannot strongly express without the utterance of a word. And his strong, well-knit and flexible frame is an engine for action than which no mortal never need desire a better.

The question is sometimes asked, is Henry Ward Beecher a handsome man? Don't *you* ask it, reader. It is a question that cannot be answered. Can any one think those heavy eyes, that indescribable nose, those pouting, I-don't-care sort of lips, that tumbled hair, that boyish face, handsome? Not very easily. *But*, can we call that glowing eye, that soul-lit face, those eloquent lips, and that royal brow, ugly—homely? Impossible! Let the question rest.

When not in "a brown study," Mr. Beecher's manners are the most free and genial that can be imagined; but every year seems to render him more and more abstracted. People are sometimes hurt and offended by his indifference and forgetfulness of them, when he is utterly unconscious of all outward things, intent upon his next sermon or lecture ; for he makes his sermons in the streets, in stores, in lumber yards, on ferry-boats, or wherever he may chance to be. And it is plain to be seen, that a man in the midst of sermon-making, cannot be very thoughtful of his manners to those who chance to pass or to pause beside him.

It is said that a polished and courteous brother clergyman one day called on Mr. Beecher ; and on being shown into his study, found him stretched upon the floor, from which he made no haste to rise. "I am studying my sermon," said Mr. Beecher, looking steadily and gravely into the fire which burned before him.

On one occasion it was thought needful that Mr. Beecher should be waited on by a committee of ministers, in order that they might reassure themselves and the churches of his sound orthodoxy. When the object of their visit was stated—"Let us pray," said Mr. Beecher instantly—"let us pray ;" and the prayer, if we mistake not, settled the matter satisfactorily.

The children like Mr. Beecher—*that* shows what his nature is. They all love to speak to him, to play with him, to hand him flowers. They crowd his pulpit stairs ; the boys gather almost about his feet. After meeting one spring evening, while Mr. Beecher was talking with several gentlemen, upon some apparently important business, a little rosy-faced girl stepped on to the platform, and holding out a bunch of white and red clover, said: "Here, Mr. Beecher." He instantly bent towards the child, and taking the flowers, said in a pleased tone, and with a kind smile: "*Thank* you; these smell like the country." The child looked perfectly delighted as she darted away. The mystery and secret of Henry Ward Beecher's wonderful success as a preacher, may be explained in his own words, which *he* applied to another: "He preaches life-truths in life-forms, with the power of his life in their utterance."

He is not a greater man, not a more learned man, not a better man, than many other ministers who never can keep people awake. But he *is* more *alive.* Why; there is intense life in all that, in desk or pulpit, he does or says. What wonder that he who is so vivid there *should* sometimes sog and smolder, when the excitement of his work is over.

Many excellent Christian people, growing anxious lest the preaching of a man whose influence must necessarily be so great and wide should be pernicious, take long journeys for the object of satisfying themselves of the truth of the matter. Hardly a Sabbath passes in which several of these intent and anxious faces cannot be seen, narrowly regarding the minister, as, all unconscious of them, he delivers his message for the day.

Although every now and then, such good people get some remark which causes them to look a little doubtful, their faces clear before the sermon is over; and when the final prayer is ended, and the final hymn sung, they go away praising God for the good that he is accomplishing through the instrumentality of the man whose influence they had feared.

The whole country knows that the singing of Plymouth Church is Congregational. It knows also that some of the hymns sung there are those that are forbidden to many orthodox and dignified churches. But too great a price is often paid for dignity. Not all the dignity on earth is worth the feelings with which the thousands of that great congregation, standing up together, sing joyfully the hymn commencing—

"Amazing grace! how sweet the sound," etc.

and its chorus (in which even the children join) of

"Oh! that will be joyful to meet to part no more."

and then listen to the parting blessing of their pastor—"And until that blessed day, to which he is bringing us on, may the blessing of God be with us; and the glory shall be given to the Father, the Son, and the Holy Ghost, Amen."

No man can be truly great whose central life-purpose is to be great. Selfish ambition is certain death to those principles which give men immortality. Love to God, or love to man, or both of these, must lie at the foundations of all true fame. For the sake of preaching the Gospel—the Gospel of redemption and of freedom—Henry Ward Beecher lives; for this sake he would die. This is his purpose; and into this work he throws all that there is in him, and all that he, by seeking throughout the height and depth of life, can obtain.

That he has stood—that he is standing—where the temptation to pride and self-conceit is strong, he knows well; and with all his heart he has besought the Lord to keep him clothed in the garments of humility. Year after year the multitudes throng him; they press around him, till the place that holds him is too strait for them. They hang upon his words, they love him, they revere him. The man is not deaf nor blind; his heart is not a stone, and it needs no philosopher to say that in his position *only* the grace of God can keep a man humble, and without any affectations of vanity. The Lord has heard the prayer of his servant. The "Mountain" knows that it is high; the "Lion" knows that he is strong. It would be mere affectation to deny that; but though he has proper self-respect, it is well proportioned and justly combined with self-abnegation. No man forgets *himself* more, or regards himself more soberly, than does Henry Ward Beecher.

This is the opposite of what was feared in the beginning of his course.

Ten—eleven years ago, when first people began to talk of the great numbers Henry Ward Beecher was drawing, there were remarks like the following made:

"It's a new thing; people will run after novelties."

"It won't last long, depend on that. These young guns burst suddenly—vanity charges them too heavily."

"Oh it's more the name of Beecher than anything else."

"He is the tail end of the heap; he never *would* study."

"Any man that has tact and boldness, and that knows how to swell, can draw a crowd for a while."

And Rev. Dr. Shepard, of the Theological Seminary in Bangor, Maine, remarked, "If Mr. Beecher continues to draw so large a congregation for six years, he will prove himself a remarkable man." And now, having seen how the matter turned, that heroic divine (heroic in the fullest sense of the word, for men who would not fear to die in battle, or to risk life in other ways, often lack heroism to stick to their post when *money* beckons them away), who excels as scholar, preacher, and critic, has become a hearty approver and admirer of Mr. Beecher. It needs no more than *this* to show that the feet of the pastor of Plymouth Church stand on firm and solid ground.

He has his faults, and they are numerous, and not too small to be seen with the naked eye. Perhaps the very reason why he so admires gentleness, is because he has not in his own disposition overmuch of that quality. But of his faults there are sufficient who are ready to speak, and to rejoice in them. Well, as he says, "There always will be persons who have in them the carrion nature." Such as their pastor is, with all his glorious powers, or with reactive dullness, with all his virtues, and with all his faults, his people love him.

They have, however, one cause of regret in regard to

him. Mr. Beecher is a sound and vigorous man, physically; but he cannot last always—he, as well as others, must die; and where is the material that shall live after him? that shall show to the future world what a man once lived and died? He is now forty-six years old, and not yet are prepared the witnesses which shall speak for him after he has gone hence. Full measure, pressed down, running over, has his life ever given; but will he be of their number whose dying is but an endless multiplying of their life? His sermons, matchless as they are, are seldom fully written out; and no mortal hand but his own can properly retouch them. Hitherto, he has not, except in one or two instances, given to the *world* proof of what he is. In his pulpit—on his own platform—he is seen and known—known to such as have listened to him often—for no man can judge of Henry Ward Beecher from one or two sermons. No crystal was ever so many sided as he; all sides so bright and pure; but abroad, where he goes to *lecture*, they neither see nor hear him. Oh! that his platform had a tongue! or better, that it knew to use the pen; then would be manifested, before all the world, the splendor and the power; the yearning love, the crushing wrath, the thunderous denunciations, the resistless appeals, the originality, the logic, the analysis, the heroism, the philosophy, which render this man unsurpassed in setting forth the truths of the Religion of Christ.

Henry Ward Beecher came of a goodly stock; Welsh blood, with its poetry and music, flows in his veins. He is indeed a poet; though it is not known that ever in his life he made one line to rhyme with another. But get him before a fine painting, and see the poetic frenzy that comes mightily upon him there.

He is not much gifted with prudence in the use of money; and is so generous towards those that have need of his aid, that, as a gentleman of his congregation remarked, when there was talk in regard to raising his salary: "Three thousand dollars a year is, as far as his own interest is concerned, just as good as ten thousand; for he has nothing, now, when the end of the year comes; and he would have no more then."

Nor are all his gifts *public* ones. To the unknown poor he does good; they who have sat in great darkness, and whom he knew but little more of than this, that they were in trouble and want, have known his ready generosity. Such persons know that it is from the impulse of his heart, and not to gain a name for benevolence, that Henry Ward Beecher does good with his money.

THE LECTURE-ROOM.

THE Lecture-room of Plymouth Church is entered from both ends, and is capable of seating about four hundred persons. Mr. Beecher's desk stands directly before the door at which he always enters. Between the desk and the door is a high and wide white screen of boards. Towards this screen all eyes are directed, from the time the people are assembled until the pastor appears. The meetings are always well attended—generally they are crowded; and better or more interesting prayer and conference meetings there are not. People flock to them with a real, living pleasure, which is printed upon their features. A sensation of gladness is always experienced when the pastor's face appears.

Taking his seat, Mr. Beecher gives out a hymn, and then calls upon some brother to pray. This is three times repeated. The hymns are not read, unless one happens to strike with peculiar force the pastor or some brother; or unless it set to ringing some "silver bell" in Mr. Beecher's heart; in which case he reads it, in his own touching manner.

After the third prayer the meeting is open for remarks; and speakers are heard from various parts of the room. The brethren make known an experience, a want, or they ask a question. Anything practical the pastor is glad to hear. "Anything," as he says, "that has life in it." And when one takes into consideration the transcendent prayer and conference-meeting aptitude of the pastor, it is really astonishing with what freedom the most halting and uneducated persons rise up, and unabashed before him, express their minds, and open their feelings.

Strangers attending the meetings are prone to think that, after hearing the pastor talk, no one else would dare to open his mouth. But Mr. Beecher's aim is to encourage and draw out the humble and stammering disciple, and in this he succeeds to admiration. The minister sits smiling in his seat, like a loved teacher; and to him both old and young submit any question of duty or of doctrine by which they are exercised. He is faithful to warn, exhort, check, or encourage; and his power of applying cures to right places seems, sometimes, well-nigh miraculous. It is a strange thing to see old, grey-headed men arise and ask that comparatively young one, of things too deep for their understanding; and stranger still is it to hear how, without a moment's hesitation, the young one pours light upon the whole subject, while the inquirer sinks to his seat silent and satisfied.

When a man stands up and begins, after a dead and formal manner, to make a long, set exhortation upon generalities, he is very liable to be requested to alter the tone of his remarks, or to make them brief. That brother will be liable to be asked if he thinks his religion renders him any more amiable than he was; if he is any more agreeable and patient in his family, any more merciful and just with his clerks, any more upright and humble in every part of his life. Such home thrusts are useful in bringing people down from that convenient generality that we "are all great sinners," from reflections and remarks that hit no one, and help no one, and they fasten attention on particular points where attention is needed.

But while canting exhortations and heartless prayers are thus discouraged, the most trembling lisper who really *has* a thing to say, and don't undertake to speak or pray merely from "a sense of duty," is kindly heard. If a timid beginner in the prayers and the language of Zion, break down in the midst of his utterance, instead of the dead and awkward, the half killing silence, made appalling to the stammerer by exchanged glances and nods, perhaps, also, by smiles from those present, the word is instantly taken up by the pastor, or by some brother, and the distress of the young convert is covered and cured.

Any one who has ever witnessed such scenes as have taken place within the last year, in some conference meetings, will know how fully to appreciate the delicacy and skill of management like this.

People accustomed but to solemn faces in prayer-meetings, are frequently shocked at seeing a smile, or hearing a sound as of subdued laughter, go round the lecture-room of Plymouth Church. Well; the charge that people laugh there cannot be denied; they *do*.

But the laughter of levity, or of trifling with things sacred, is not that which Mr. Beecher's remarks excite, and he holds the strange belief that man was made to laugh, when he feels like it, even in the presence of God himself. And if there is a man or woman with a face so stiff as not to smile, or laugh outright, at the sudden and skillful hits made by Mr. Beecher at various faults and errors, surely it is not one that would be welcomed everywhere with love and joy.

Laughter thus caused has oftentimes more power to send an evil into annihilation than twenty years of grim and solemn argumentation would have.

A nickname well applied can paint a man better than any brush of artist. "Go tell that *Fox*," says Jesus, and what labored description could set Herod more vividly before us?

It is a fact that Mr. Beecher *cannot* keep his face to that devout measure and expression which those who gravely censure him, so holily wear.

The people smile at their pastor, and at each other, and he smiles at them. Thus there is sunshine at evening there. Anon they look at him with falling tears, and his own eyes fill, and the tears roll down as he speaks of Christ's love and pity, or of man's ingratitude. Certainly, if it is better to suppress all such signs of feeling, it is more painful, and those who sit side by side unmoved, while are poured the prayer, the song, the entreaty, *cannot* love each other as *they* do who have, in their meetings, looked through smiles and tears, through sorrow and laughter, into each other's very hearts.

Since the coming hither of Dr. Lyman Beecher the meetings have often been more interesting than ever. He stands like a glorious old ruin, speaking of the good days of the past. And he utters a few words more of love and invitation to the world before he leaves its shores forever.

How ardently he loved his work! how he loves it now!

One night the subject of remark during conference was "Looking unto Jesus." Mr. Beecher, with his usual power, had illustrated this looking, by the looking of a child towards its parents, a soldier to his officer, etc., and had then proceeded to show how much greater encouragement one would take by looking unto Christ. Said he, "'Tis hard to make people habitually do this, but far harder to cause them to realize that Jesus is *actually* always looking upon *them.* I think that more Christians, and the same one for a greater number of times, take comfort by what they do towards the Lord, than by what the Lord does towards them. We know that we do, sometimes at least, look upwards, lovingly, confidingly; but that he looks down on us with real, throbbing love, we can't seem to believe *that.* There are many reasons why this seems impossible. Our own consciousness of ill desert, our meanness, our coldness, our entire unloveliness, all appear to stand in the way of our being objects of *love* to him. Yet it was against this very feeling that he aimed his discourse in the chapter where he asks if an earthly parent will give his child a stone for bread, or a serpent for a fish, etc. We say, "Oh, of course, an earthly parent would not deal so; he must love his offspring, but God is different; he is so far off, so much above us; there may be reasons why he cannot regard us."

Nay, but Christ twists the argument *the other way.* "If *ye,* BEING EVIL, know how to give good gifts, etc. Is it because your child is good, and does all things to please you, that you give of your fullness to him? Or is it because he is *your own,* and you *love* him? Now you reach it, that is the manner of feeling which God has for all who once and heartily have given themselves to him. But don't you think that your poor, unsteady and imperfect love is more true and enduring than his. Out of his infinite goodness his love flows to us; the reasons for it are in his own nature, not in ours."

Here the venerable Dr. Beecher rose and said: "I want to say one thing about this looking of God. There must always be something to look at."

He sat down. It was plain that the watchful Father in Zion feared that, from some omission in his son's remarks, the ignorant and foolish might take occasion to think, "We will do evil that *love* may abound."

Mr. Beecher had been sitting in his chair, as his manner is when he speaks often, and but a few moments at a time, in the meetings; but now he rose and moved aside his table. Bending forward over the edge of his platform, he said, "I should like to know what He saw to look at when he so loved the world that he gave himself to die for it. When a man's back is towards God, and he is hating him, I don't think that God ever sees that man's face. Even for such persons God's love is compassionate, though it cannot be the peculiar affection one feels for his own child; but the moment that the man's face is turned towards God, the love of a father to his son is but a feeble sign of the infinite tenderness with which the Almighty Father regards him. It is the world that needs to be reconciled, not God."

"That is just what I meant," said old Mr. Beecher.

"I knew you did, father; but I wanted them to understand it in my words too."

At another time, Dr. Beecher hearing a blind brother, who rather inclined to the doctrine of perfection, make some remarks to the effect that the way of perfection was the way of peace, remarked: "If we are to have no peace, and no sense of justification, until we do love the Lord with *all* our heart, and soul, and strength, and until we are conscious that we are free from offences, no man who knows his own heart can *ever* have them. The love of God is with his children the paramount love, but never, till they get to heaven, will it be all that the command requires. Measuring ourselves by the law of absolute perfection, every man falls short every day. There are two sorts of perfection by which God's creatures stand: one, the perfection of absolute obedience; the other, the perfection of faith. By the first the angels stand, by the last stands man. *Faith* is counted to us for righteousness. Faith is shown by love and good works, but both of these are imperfect, and accepted only for Jesus' sake."

"My father," said Henry Ward, "is like an old war-horse. They say that he has served his time, and they shut him into a rich pasture to take his ease for the rest of his days. But he *won't* take his ease; he scorns it. When the trumpet sounds the pasture cannot hold him; he leaps the fence, and takes his old place in the ranks, marching with the rest until the parade is over. And you cannot keep father away from the work to which his life was so freely and earnestly given." Again he said: "My father has made his journey and reached the shore; but he is waiting for a little time before he crosses, to call back to those that are still upon the way, and to tell them of the things that shall make their journeying less toilsome and dangerous. He will go over soon."

"I waited to see *one more revival*," exclaimed the old gentleman in a lively tone. "I have seen it—a glorious one. It is the beginning of the end. God will show you greater things than these. In the four churches over which I was pastor there were four years of revival. Revivals never ought to stop. I am willing to wait twenty more years if I can be permitted to work in a revival."

The glad times during the great revival of 1857–8 seemed to renew the youth of Dr. Beecher.

"This meeting," said Mr. Beecher at one time, "is the bellows which keeps the fire going, yonder in the Great Congregation. I am sure that more depends upon it than upon the Sunday service—at least without it the preaching would be almost powerless. This is a pleasant place—we all love it. I think that we can say, that here we have spent some of the happiest hours of our whole lives."

NOTES

FROM PLYMOUTH PULPIT.

There are two views of the Gospel, *both of which* some churches use.

One view of it is, that it is a power which makes laws for the protection of all men who will quietly yield up their rights, and submit themselves to what will inevitably crush out of them their manhood.

The other view is, that the Gospel is a power which secures to man all the inherent rights of his nature, and which protects him in them.

The first view regards men as mere passive bricks for the building of the palace of society, which is considered the important thing. The latter view considers society as the school for training individual men.

Man is the most important thing created on the earth. Rulers, societies and systems are but his servants and protectors.

The churches are welcome to which one of

these views they like best. They shall not have both. I take the latter side, and declare that those who don't believe in it had better stop sending out Bibles. They had better stop ministers, at any rate such ones as I am; for I preach *knowing* that the Gospel is a bombshell in the midst of thrones, and a mine beneath every fortress of power whose strength is used against the people's rights instead of for them.

TAKE from the Bible the Godship of Christ, and to me it would be but a heap of dust. I would as soon have all Egypt raked into a heap, wherein not a stone of its cities, nor a trace of its inhabitants could be found, as that book if its Christ be not God.

MAN is required to pour all that is in him—*all* of his life and love—into the bosom of Christ; and when that is done, what is there left for God?

THE man who, after having cast his care on Christ, goes to fretting and worrying himself about anything or anybody, is like one who, having purchased a through ticket from here to—anywhere, and receiving a check for his baggage, gets out of the car at the end of a mile or two, and, shouldering his trunk, starts to go the rest of the way alone. Christ never rolls back upon us burdens that we lay on him; we take them back ourselves. What is a religion worth that will stay with a man in the sunshine, but clear out in a storm? The Christian has a right, and it is his duty, to be free from all care and anxiety. Let him lie on the promises, and be at rest. "Oh! but," says the doubting, worrying disciple, "the promises are made to the righteous; and I am so full of imperfections I dare not claim them." Well, brother, if you wait for that righteousness which is by the law, you'll *never* be able to rest on the promises; but if you trust in Christ, *that* is counted to you for righteousness; and your right to the comfort of the promises is as good as though you were as holy as an angel. Christ's love sweeps away the unworthiness of all who sincerely love him. God has undertaken for you; trust him, though you know not where to get your next supply of bread.

THAT Christ does not hold men to proper and unselfish motives when they come to him for healing, we may see by the cleansing of the nine selfish and ungrateful lepers. He knew their dispositions and motives, as well before as after he had granted their prayer. God *allows* men to cry out to him from selfish fear; and he never refuses to attend to any earnest cry. If he did not attend to such cries, or receive such persons, whom would he receive? Dare any man lift up his face and say, "When *I* cried unto God, I cried worthily, from pure and disinterested motives." The conditions are not "Come with pure hearts and motives unto me;" they are "Come, and your motives shall afterwards be made right." A true conversion will do that work. Nothing else will. If you are awake to your danger, if you see, at last, that your only hope is in Jesus, don't stop to examine your motives, or his willingness to receive you just as you are. Rush to his feet this moment. All that you cannot do, he can and will do. All that you *now* have to do is heartily to *come*. Drop every hope and every dependence but Christ, and give your whole life and soul into his keeping.

A TEAR, dropped in the silence of a sick chamber, often rings in heaven with a sound which belongs not to earthly trumpet or bells.

GOD is more willing to give good gifts unto them that ask him, than men are to give them unto their children! God could not have struck the foundation note of human desire squarer than he did by this declaration.

There is no honor toward God, either in the heart of man or woman. Suppose that I dared to go into a school and take some young maiden—one the least hackneyed in the ways of life, and, calling upon her the attention of all her companions and teachers, declare that her soul was base, mean and vulgar; that she was without natural affection or human feeling; that she regarded not the good of brother nor sister, and that she returned the affection of father and mother with ingratitude and contempt. Why! she would not for a moment bear such charges—she would die—she would suffocate with shame. Yet I stand here and I charge upon you young maidens, and young men—upon every one of you into whose eyes I look, if you have not given your hearts to Christ, conduct infinitely worse than this; because 'tis towards one who is more to you than any earthly friend can possibly be. I charge upon you the meanest, the most base and unnatural conduct that can be imagined; but you sit calmly under *that*, you look me in the face and do not blush, and not a feeling of shame stirs in you, solely because this atrocious behavior is maintained towards God!

I think that the outreaching of God's heart of love has more power in it than the beating of God's mark has. Love is mightier than indignation.

It makes a difference to God how we act. His happiness is affected by the conduct of his children; for his heart is the heart of a father. If, when my child sins, a pang goes through my own soul, and I fly to rescue him from further iniquity, it is because God struck into my breast a little spark of what in him is infinite.

Some men are, in regard to ridicule, like tin-roofed buildings, in regard to hail—all that hits them bounds rattling off, not a stone goes through.

Christ never stands rebuking before he pardons and helps the suppliant.

God hates sin, because it destroys what he loves. He could live high and lifted up above all noise of man's groaning—all smoke of his torment; but his nature is to come down after man—to grope for him amid all the dark pollutions of sin, and if possible, to rescue and cleanse him.

God hates sin very much as mothers hate wild beasts. One day a woman stood washing beside a stream. She was in a wild, frontier country, and the woods were all around. Her little, only child was playing about near her. By and by she missed the infant's prattle, and looking about her called its name. There was no answer. Alarmed, the mother ran to the house, but her babe was not there. In wild distress the poor woman now fled to search the woods, and there she found her child. But it was only its little *body* that she clasped to her heart. A wolf had seized her treasure, and when, at last, she rescued it from those bloody fangs, its spirit had gone. Oh! how that mother hated wolves!! And do you know that this is the very figure Christ uses to show what feeling he has towards the sin that is seeking to devour his children?

When we sin we are not going against a cold, unfeeling law; but are striking, with cruel hand, direct at the living, loving heart of God.

"This loving God," you say; "I can't do it. How can I love infinity—omnipotence? I might as well try to love a cloud, or to try to embrace in my warm palpitating affections the vast expanse of ether." True, you cannot love God—you cannot love this expansive, mysterious essence of omnipotence. God knows very well that you cannot, and for that reason among others, he condescended to bring himself down to your capacity; to come within the reach of your affections in the person of Jesus Christ. "God *manifest* in the flesh." From my soul I pity that man who goes behind Christ and seeks to fasten himself upon God unrevealed. As you say, he may as well seek to embrace with warm love the elastic and invisible air. But it is with Christ that we have to do, and if you *desire* to fashion him to your mind that your heart may love him, I will tell you how. Sit down and read his life—not in parts; not a chapter one day, and another the next; nor a paragraph with your coat and hat at your elbow, ready to start for New York; but read his life straight through, giving your mind and your heart time to take in the meaning of what you read. Thus you may view him in his loveliness, and your affections cannot fail of being touched. If you went into an artist's studio to look at the picture of some distinguished person of whose appearance you wished to get a clear idea, how do you think it would answer to have, at your first visit, all of that painted face except the forehead, covered? Looking at that a little while, you go away and come again the following day. The forehead is covered now, and the lower parts of the face, but the eyes are visible. You look at them a few moments and go away as before. The next day they give you a view of the nose, exclusively; the next you behold the upper lip; next they give you the lower lip, and finally the chin. Now you have seen the whole face; but do you know how it looks? No, you don't. You can form no idea of the effect of such a combination of features; you can't imagine what the expression of the face is, you don't know it from Adam's. Now, who would for a moment put up with such portrait seeing? We say when we come up before a picture: "Get out of the way—let me see the whole effect of this." But it is in this dissected manner that men look at the character of Christ. Not so do they study Washington; nor any other man of whose character they wish to form an opinion, and of whose personal deserts they wish to judge. Why should Christ be so unjustly treated? Did it ever occur to you that there are four lives of Christ, each one written by men of different minds, that all forms of minds might be suited? Study those lives *by the whole*, and you will find how to love him.

'Tis not safe for any man, whether Christian or not, to measure himself by any other than God's own rule. Let him draw near to God, and let him judge of himself by how he looks *there*. Let him hold up in the light of God's word the thoughts and intents of his inmost soul.

Perfect love casteth out fear. While the heart is filling, the agitations of fear remain; but, when the lake is filling by the moon-drawn and star-drawn tides, what commotion is there in its bosom—how the sands are swept about, how the muddy bottom sends its rile through all the waters. There are ripples and eddies, and struggling currents; there is seething and boiling; there are bubbles and foam, until the lake is almost filled. But as the waters deepen, as the banks grow less and less, the agitation subsides. The sand settles, the foam is blown away, the bubbles are scattered. And when the lake is filled to its utmost capacity it clears itself, and lies unruffled and serene, reflecting in its calm bosom, the moon, the stars, and the tranquil heavens. Thus is it with the heart of man. When love ebbs low in his soul he is tossed and whirled by the agitations and torments of fear; but when the Spirit of God flows in and fills his heart with divine love, the tumults are stilled; and looking up with confidence and joy, the man reflects from his overflowing soul the image of his God and Father.

Farmers have learned a lesson which many moralists have not learned; namely, that when seed is sown grain must be looked for at the latter end of the harvest, and not at the beginning.

CHRIST reveals himself unto his own in ten thousand ways, but often they do not know him when he comes. Many times he speaks to them when they do not even suspect that they have had a revelation. They dare not think it; they fear that it would be a lack of humility to believe that the Saviour really has made good his promise, and come unto them. When we are burdened and cast down, how often does some passage of Scripture dart suddenly into our mind, lighting up all our darkness like a flash from Heaven? It *is* from Heaven. Christ thus reveals himself to strengthen and encourage us. We may be beset by sore temptations, and just upon the point of yielding, when the word of warning comes; or we may be feeling desolate and forsaken, having none to lean upon, and yet not knowing how to stand alone, when the revelation has been of love that passeth understanding—of pity deep as the bosom of Almighty God. I sat once under a tree near a little stream, holding in my hands a bunch of flowers. Suddenly, from the air came swooping down upon them a little bird. He had not seen me; when he did so he instantly fled: but he could not take from me the sweet surprise and the exciting pleasure of his visit. Thus comes flying to us the new revelation from our God. New in effect, though old in letter. Like the bird that only touched me with its little feet and bill, it may but alight a moment on our heart, and depart as suddenly as it came, but it does its work. As, at a touch from some passing thing, the dew-laden bushes shake off at morn the weight of the burden that has been pressing down all their leaves, so, at one shock, do our hearts shake off their burdens, and rise up in thanksgiving and joy.

A MAN who is very much afraid of sins that bring immediate shame and punishment, while he cares nothing at all for those which are of a nature to recur, increase and form character, is like a child who should come laughing into a room with his apron full of asps; but be very much terrified at being chased by a butterfly.

THERE is no enduring happiness apart from God. As well might a branch broken from a tree in the forest say, "Now I am free—I will grow and be a tree by myself," as any human soul say, "I will be free—I will do as I like and be happy in my own way," when he does not draw on God for his enjoyment. He is a broken bough—a reed plucked up; a waif floating no whither. True happiness he can never know until he comes to draw it from its only source—God.

There are sins which, like asps, always carry their sting with them. The instant one meddles with them, he is struck by the poisoned dart. Such sins are generally rare and admitted to be very wrong. But there are others that are far more dangerous. Men in tropical climates may be very much afraid of tigers; but there are multitudes of minute insects flying in the woods whose bite is death. Shall they be less afraid of these?

Men often hunger and thirst after God when they don't know what ails them. There is cradled in every man's soul, though often nearly smothered, something which is the child of God, ever crying out for its Father. You may say, "I cast religion, priests and churches overboard; I'll have no more to do with them, I've seen through them, and they are worthless." But you *will* have more to do with them, for when you have destroyed the outward forms, the living want will still be in you. Religion is not a thing of arbitrary requisitions it is an inherent need of the soul. The Bible and ordinances are but evoked by man's necessities, to help him. You come to church, you think your cheeks are hard, and they *are;* you think your hearts are hard, and they *are* hard; you think you can resist the dogmas, and so you can; therefore I shall not present them. I won't throw pearls before swine, but being crafty, I catch you with guile. Many of you are ashamed that you want to come here; some of you go out cursing because your hearts are touched. But you come again and again. You are what is called gospel hardened; but in reality you are word hardened. You have heard the same things presented in the same way so long that you are tired of them; therefore I go out of my way to get new forms in which to present old truths. For your sakes I forsake all set rules of sermonizing, and strike direct at that within you which I *know* will echo to my words. I know that in every man's bosom there is that which at times longs for something better and purer than he is. At your interior consciousness I aim my thrust. I strike my blow. Those old bells in you, I will make them ring. You may turn out the sexton, you may cut off the rope. I'll throw stones and hit your bells if I can do nothing more. To the truth they shall peal out, and your soul shall tremble at the peal.

JOURNALS are often the devil's vanity trap. Men write in them pretending to themselves that they don't expect them to be published, when all the time they know that they will be; and are writing under the influence of that idea.

In some waters a man may drive strong piles and build his warehouses upon them, sure that the waters are not powerful enough to undermine his foundations; but there is an innumerable army of minute creatures at work beneath the water, feeding themselves upon those strong piles. They gnaw, they bore, they cut, they dig, into the solid wood, and at last a child might overthrow those foundations, for they are cut through and eaten to a honeycomb. Thus by avarice, revenge, jealousy and selfishness, men's dispositions are often cut through and they don't know it.

There are men who delight to see evil in those professing godliness. They doubt, they leer, they jeer. Well, there are birds appointed to seek for carrion, and they always find it. By their very seeking they declare their own nature. Don't you imitate their dirty flight. They are of the carrion family.

God values men according to what they have had to walk through. Some men are so made that they are obliged to hold perpetual warfare with themselves. They must have a hand always on the engine, or something will blow up in them every minute.

There are doubts and troubles that never can be settled. The only thing to be done with them is to lay them down and leave them. This the Christian must do if he wants peace; and if the impenitent won't do it they will torment him to death. That's all he'll gain by clinging to them. There is no system by which everything can be made to look clear to men while they live in the flesh. As long as we live there must continue to be many things that to us seem dark and mysterious. It matters not. Enough that there is no darkness, no mystery which is not clear to God. To him let us trust matters, and not take the care of things upon ourselves.

God will certainly take care of you if you bear your whole weight on him. He may not do it just in your way; but he will do it. He cannot let one of your real interests perish, or be hurt, without the most dreadful perjury of himself.

Great crimes ruin comparatively few. It is the little meannesses, selfishnesses, and impurities, that do the work of death on most men; and these things march not to the sound of fife or drum. They steal with muffled tread, as the foe steals on the sleeping sentinel.

What a man *has* thought and felt bears intimate relation to what he *now* thinks and feels. There is no such thing as divesting one's self of the influences of former living. A man's life is a concatenation—he is rolled over and over on himself.

There are many men who have a dyspepsia of books.

In love, the freshness and charm of youth have caught men's attention, and they have pronounced the first love best; but it is the poorest. One does not know how to love till he has felt the discipline of life. Young love is a flame; very pretty, often very hot and fierce, but still only light and flickering. The love of the older and disciplined heart is as coals, deep-burning, unquenchable.

A realization of the spiritual nature and the eternal duration of man purifies and elevates our social intercourse. The clearer a man sees man's destination and true life, the more he reveres humanity as a thing sacred and honored of God.

I don't believe in definitions of feelings or classes of feelings. They can be illustrated—not defined

There is a time when one is neither one thing nor another; not exactly in boyhood, and not exactly in manhood, but in the limbo of vanity. This is the time when parents become foolish, and not worth minding; when the theology of one's childhood becomes bigotry, narrow, simple; when one yearns for largeness, liberty. This is the time of danger. Infidelity with dark wing hovers near, and if the youth be not now guided wisely and betimes they become its victims. Having myself narrowly escaped this doom, I know how to sympathize with those who are in danger.

Reason is like a telescope—you can arrange it so that with it you can see only the things near to you, but it has other powers. By drawing it out and properly adjusting the glasses, you can make what is near you to grow dim, and the things far off to come near, and by and by, when the lenses are all right, you can see beyond the stars and into the heavenly city, and the magnificent background to your view is the glory of God.

Suffering rightly borne weakens that part of us that should be weak, and strengthens what should be strong.

WILL men's prayers be answered? Not if they pray as boys whittle sticks, absently, hardly knowing or caring what they are about. I've known men to begin to pray about Adam, and go on from him away down to the present time, whittling their stick clear to a point with about as much feeling, and doing about as much good as the boy does.

REFINEMENT is one of the outworkings of faith in the spiritual. It is the lifting of one's self upwards from the merely sensual, the effort of the soul to etherealize the common wants and uses of life. A really refined man who ignores Christianity is a creature to beget wonder. A man whose sense of color is so exquisite that one wrong shade cannot escape his eye, that harmony of hues is his soul's delight, I marvel that *that* man's eye has never pierced the blue, and caught the sparkle of the gems that glow with matchless dyes upon the gates of the eternal city. A man whose ear is all attuned to melody, who has brought music to its highest earthly perfection, and stands entranced by the sweetness of its passing tones, I marvel that *he* never hears the ringing of the harps of heaven. And he who has lifted his affections until no touch of grossness ever defiles them, who has made them pure as crystal from the taint of life's vulgarity, I marvel, more and more, that along their edges plays no fire from the celestial treasury of love—that as the lightning from the earth leaps forth and joins and mingles with the lightning from the cloud, his love is not touched and intensified by the love of God. What rapine! what havoc! when such an one—his life being touched—goes forth, naked and alone, to find that he has stopped infinitely short of any preparation which could make the happiness of Heaven possible to him.

Men who concentrate themselves all upon one point may be sharp, acute, pungent—they may have spear-like force of character, but they are never broad and round, never of full-proportioned manhood; which can only be obtained by the carrying forward of the whole of a man in an even-breasted march.

Many a man never sees into heaven, till he sees there through the grave of his little child, or till he loses his wife, not only the better half, but often the whole better part of himself. That unutterable loss which darkens the house, which darkens life itself; which takes the breath out of the years, and leaves a man to go staggering through the world, like one smitten at noonday with blindness.

To some it is appointed to wander in Gethsemane, having no variation to their lives except a walk over to Calvary. There are faces lifted up to me from this congregation, into which I cannot look without revelations of their owners' peculiar histories, which seem like flashes from another world. They sit calm and still before me; but I know that no scorpions or vipers can sting as they are stung through every one of their best affections. Every day their tears fall. For years and years they have borne this, and yet they can bear witness that through faith they have been enabled to endure. More; that though they expect no relief, faith will support them to the end. Is religion, then, a fantasy, when it can so uphold the soul amid all the waves of trouble? I tell you *no*. Let who chooses to do so, swelter in philosophical anguish; I prefer to stand serene upon my Christian faith and hope. You may scoff at it and call it folly. I tell you it is *a very comfortable thing* to find refuge from every distressful and corroding care in the love of God.

I THINK no man could have his arm rot and drop away, from wrist to shoulder, and not know it; but you shall find numberless men whose *consciences* have rotted, from circumference to core, and they know nothing about it. They are less concerned about themselves than when the corruption first began. This *silence* of the hollowing out of a man—this noiseless process of preparing him for destruction, is an element of very great fearfulness. It fills me with grief and sadness, as I look on men, to know that as the snow falls, flake by flake, and no sound tells of its accumulation—that as the dust sifts in, and no noise warns of its choking rise, so silently, so surely, man is heaping to himself wrath against the day of wrath, and does not know it.

SHE was a woman, and by so much nearer to God as that makes one.

LIVE not for selfish aims. Live to shed joy on others. Thus best shall your own happiness be secured; for no joy is ever given freely forth that does not have quick echo in the giver's own heart.

EVERY action of the intellect, save that which is purely scientific, is based upon some *feeling*. Ambition says to intellect, "Look out for me;" fear cries "Look out for me." Greed also, "Arouse, sharpen yourself; pierce the darkness, teach me how to gain;" and love cries passionately, pleadingly, "Awake, be my advocate, think, think for me."

NEITHER I nor my family ever put on the garments of mourning. I will not permit it. Yet I would not refuse to those who think differently from me, the right to change their garments in memory of their beloved dead. But do not borrow of the devil; choose some color that shall speak of hope, of release, of victory. Draw not over yourselves the black tokens of pollution. Do not blaspheme by naming that despair which is triumph and eternal life.

"THEREFORE let no man glory in men, for all things are yours. Whether Paul, or Apollos, or Cephas, or the world, or life, or death, or things present, or things to come, all are yours, and ye are Christ's, and Christ is God's." This is a wonderful ownership; nowhere else in the world is there such an one. The time is coming when even to the grosser property of earth this will apply; for the heirs of heaven are not to be forever the paupers of earth; but now it is true of all things pertaining to the realm of mind. The things our Father made are ours, not in the sense of our having any right to deprive others of them, but ours as our earthly father's home and goods were ours in the days of our childhood. Were not our parents, our brothers and sisters, was not the infant sleeping in its cradle, ours? Was not the shelter of the roof-tree ours?

Was not the homestead ours? Were not the fields, the gardens, the trees, the flowers, ours, in the full heart-possession, which is the interior, the true ownership. Were they not just as sensibly our own as though we alone possessed them? And were they not ours because we were the children of our father? And were they any the *less* ours because they belonged to our brothers just the same? If we are the children of God, we are the owners of all the good things in the universe. Read here the title; it has our Father's seal. We read of the noble ones, the mighty and holy ones of old, and we say: "These men are ours—They know it now, for they are where the light is clear, and ere many days they will give us loving welcome.

We stand before the gifted, refined, and noble men of our own time; they do not know or heed us, but they are ours, as we are theirs, and soon we shall rejoice together in the glad possession. We walk among the well-known princes of reform and progress. They have an influence over us, that we cannot resist—they make us laugh or weep—they steal our hearts, they direct our thoughts, but they regard us not amid the crowds that flock to hear them. They do not see or know their brothers, but we know *them* right well, and we bide our time; eternity is long—there is no haste there—no overwork, no weariness, and no indifference or misinterpretation, and those great, rich souls shall yet acknowledge and receive us. We are among them now, as a disguised man in his father's house. He sees his parents and his brethren, and he is happy to be with them, though they know him not. He knows them well, and he can afford to wait awhile until they discover him. The Christian who lives near to God, finds a fulfillment of the promise that whoever for Christ's sake forsakes aught, shall receive in this world many fold more than he loses. But oh! that world to come! that world eternal which is also ours! Why should any Christian feel himself poor? I believe there is no feeling more universal in the human heart than that of loneliness. At the outset of life every face glows; every heart has its high hopes, and no one thinks much of the insufficiency of the things of time; but when the middle hours of life draw on, not more than one-third of the faces are still bright—two-thirds are disappointed and almost discouraged. When the evening comes, not more than one in a thousand carries the light still in his eye and on his forehead. The nine hundred and ninety-nine have fallen by the way. They have tasted the cold selfishness of the world; their breasts and their sides have been pierced by the jagged points and the poisoned thorns against which rude winds and struggling waves, have dashed them.

They have felt the utter insufficiency of human help and sympathy; and it has been well for them, if instead of lying down in the bitterness of despair, they have turned for what they so greatly needed to the only fountain of availing sympathy and aid. "Alone! alone!" has been and is the wail of every human heart that has not been satisfied by the love of God. And the Christian, while on earth, is subject to seasons of the same distress, when he will feel unknown, unloved, forsaken of his kind. But he knows that 'tis only for a moment that his desolation can endure, and then he will enter where all are his, and where they all will own him. *Then*, when he walks with wings and not with feet, he may measure his possessions, and never again will his heart be cold, or lone, or sad.

To some men the mere fact of existence, the simple walking through the air and light, gives more pleasure than others find in the whole round of so-called pleasures.

PAUL was converted as the germ of a peach sprouts. It splits its shell clear off, and has free room to root and grow. Many conversions only crack the shell; and it is worn so long that the man's Christian character is stunted and shallow for his whole life.

To live altogether in the affections is not safe. Death will overleap the fold, and bear away the precious lambs that are therein; and then the man will go wailing through the world, shorn of all that was life to him. A man's life should not "consist in the abundance of the things that he possesseth."

We are all writing books—histories of our own lives, and we can omit nothing, soften nothing. Only the naked truth can be marked upon those pages.

Let your sorrows, when they rise and swell, be like the waves of the Sound, when they at night flash forth their glories of phosphorescent light—or like the clouds that reflect the sunlight glorified.

It is a bad thing to live exclusively in taste and refinement. It begets a very wicked sort of selfishness. The man who lives too much in these faculties will be perpetually stumbling upon things shocking to his feelings, for God forgot to polish all the rocks in this world. He didn't mako trees all smooth. There are a thousand things that he didn't put velvet on. It's a pity men should grow too refined to keep company with God in his providences.

I WILL declare the whole counsel of God; I will make it to bear hardest and hottest, and to cast its light strongest and clearest on the most open and obstinate sins. I will bring it down hissing hot upon the hydra-headed monster, that many think it best to pat and soothe. I will, while the Lord spares my breath, cry aloud, and loudest when men would fain teach me prudent silence, "Woe unto them that decree unrighteous decrees; that turn aside the needy from judgment; that take away the right of the poor; that make widows their prey; that rob the fatherless; that oppress the poor to increase their riches. Behold, the hire of the laborers who have reaped down your fields, which is of you kept back by fraud, crieth; and the cries of them which have reaped are entered into the ears of the Lord of Sabaoth. Ye have lived in pleasure on the earth, and been wanton; ye have condemned and killed the just, and he doth not resist you; but, behold, the judge standeth before the door."

TEARS often prove the telescope by which men see far into heaven.

CHRISTIAN graces are natural faculties which have blossomed under the influence of divine love.

Sorrows are like clouds, which, though black when they are just passing over us, when they *are* overpast, become as if they were the garments of God thrown off in purple and gold along the horizon.

Merchants who play at snatch and grab, or at pinch and squeeze games, have need to be taught the first principles of the Gospel.

This world is like a battle-field full of little hills and hollows; and to each soldier in the war, the small valley where *he* fights seems the whole, or at least the chief part of the field. He cannot see the contest on the other side of the hill; and he thinks, in his small judgment, that as go things in his hollow, so goes the whole battle. Thus either his defeat or his victory looks to him of far more consequence than it really is. But God looks at things by the whole, and in heaven he will show them so to us. When we have fought long in a good cause, and have been at last thrown away backward, and lie gasping, perchance dying, upon our banners, we must not think that the good cause has failed. God's work never goes backward. He takes the large view of things, and when we are come up out of the blood and dust of conflict, he will show it to us, and we shall be comforted. For all that I know to be right and good I shall do battle till I die. For the encouragement and sympathy I have met, I thank God. I thank God also for the contumely and abuse which bad men have heaped upon me. It is no honor to be praised by the selfish and evil man, and the oppressor; but I would that my brethren, the sons of my Father, my fellow workers in the vineyard of the Lord, understood and loved me. But in one thing I am superior to my brother ministers who call me so bad a minister: I know that many of them are good and true men, though over careful and most mistaken ones, and I know that they have, sooner or later, got to own *me* for a good man. They are mine. They cannot help themselves. I love all that is good in them; and *they have got to love me.* There is no escape for them, "for all things are mine, and I am Christ's, and Christ is God's." Does any one ask for the full meaning of this threefold heart enshrinement? They cannot have the exposition from mortal lips; but we shall all learn its meaning when we get to heaven.

ONCE I thought of heaven with the cold rigid thoughts of the old teaching. It was a stately, solemn, unnatural place, full of everlasting practising in music. But now I take the liberty of prophecy. I see that when the oriental saints, or when Christ himself described that glorious place, they made use of whatever of earthly beauty and glory seemed greatest to those to whom they were speaking as images of it. I do the same. Every one may do the same. There is in heaven what will more than satisfy every mind. As a place for studying mathematics it could attract Newton, but I fear that I should hardly want to go there if that were to be the employment of all. But for my nature there will be abundant food, and for your natures, too, all various as they are. There is not a day passes over me here, that I do not sicken at some unworthiness or hypocrisy; but I think "Yonder there can enter nothing that defileth, or that maketh a lie." Not a day but that tears start to my eyes at the sight of other's tears; but I know that *there* "there shall be no more sorrow, nor crying." Here, I shrink daily from the contact of those that are mean and sordid; there, all is noble and generous. Here, I am often chilled by want of affection; there, all is love, perfect and undefiled. Of whatever is most beloved by me; of all that is most grand and glorious; of all that is most warm, winning and delightful, I can think and yet be sure that I have not risen to a tithe of the warmth and beauty of the glorious home awaiting the sons of God—the joint heirs of Jesus Christ.

There is scarce a time when men meet together, when they could not, if they listened for it, hear the sharp, shrill singing of ten thousand petty bees buzzing around them. Men have violated truth so long, that they have come to lie almost unconsciously.

A man's religion is not a thing all made in heaven, and then let down, and shoved into him. It is his own conduct and life. A man has no more religion than he acts out in his life.

"Take no thought for the morrow," that is, no anxious, fretful thought. Walk through to-day as well as you can, and God will undertake for your future. When you go forward out of to-day, to worry about it, you are over the fence, you are trespassing, and God will scourge you back into your own lot. When I have been fishing in a mountain stream, I have always found that so long as I kept a short line I could manage my fishing very well; but when I let my line run out, the stream took it down, and there I was, at the mercy of every stick that stuck up in the stream, and every rock that jutted out from the banks. I lost my fish and I tangled my line; very likely I lost my footing also, and got over head and ears in the stream. Now, most men have cast out their line into life *forty years long*, when it ought to be but *one day* long. In consequence, they are not able to manage their tackle at all; but are pulled after it, stumbling first into this hole, and then into that; slipping up here, and slipping down there, struggling and splashing about in far more distressed fashion than the fish at the other end of the line—and, as a general thing, there is no fish there. Haul in your line!!

BEFORE men we stand as opaque beehives. They can see the thoughts go in and out of us; but what work they do inside of a man they cannot tell. Before God we are as *glass* beehives, and all that our thoughts are doing within us he perfectly sees and understands.

CAUTION and conservatism are expected of old age; but when the young men of a nation are possessed of such a spirit, when *they* are afraid of the noise and strife caused by the new applications of the truth, Heaven save the land! Its funeral bell has already rung.

CHRISTIANS who are forever living on their own experiences, are like a leaf which has got into an eddy in the river, where it keeps whirling round and round in its own track. You shall see it there, whirling; and shall go away and sleep, and in the morning you shall come again and find the leaf there still. At noon there it is, and when night comes it is still nothing but whirl, whirl, whirl. Working, travelling, hard enough, to be sure, but making no progress. Now, let something break it loose from that whirlpool, and away it will go, merrily down the stream. Too much looking backward and inward is bad for piety and progression.

THE assertion that the "common people" heard Christ gladly, seems to imply that the higher classes cared but little for him.

THE Bible don't pretend to teach fully of anything save man's lost condition, and of his way of returning to God. The truth of it is not a subject for logic; it can only be tested by consciousness and experience. To test the truth of a Christian's experience try the life of a Christian. Go on your knees before God. Bring all your idols, bring self-will, and pride, and every evil lust before him, and give them up. Devote yourself, heart and soul, to his will and *see* if you do not "*know* of the doctrine."

This is the only way to examine, and study into Bible truths; and none that ever tried this way till their hearts grew warm with love to Christ ever had much trouble about doubting the truths of revelation. There are men who are avowedly trying to get rid of the Bible, and there are other men who sorrowfully fear that it must be given up. But destroy it, and what then?

Why we should be like men who had burned up all the wills and title deeds which would have given them a large estate—or, like sick and wounded men, who had destroyed all the means of relief. Suppose that the wounded men in the Crimean hospitals had raised an insurrection. Suppose that one man, having lost a leg, had said to another who had lost an arm, and to another with a part of his head and features shot away: "Come, let us take no more of this medicine. Let us put an end to the directions and attentions of these doctors and nurses;" and suppose that then the poor wretches had hobbled up and turned all their kind and skillful physicians out of doors; had ejected Florence Nightingale after them, and flung the nurses and the medicines, and all the surgeon's instruments out of the windows. Would all this have done them any good?

They would thus have got rid of all who could have helped them, but while the doctors, and nurses, and the remedies and balm for the wounds, were all outside of the walls, the wounds and putrifying sores, the burning anguish and tormenting pain would all have continued within.

But what is a Crimean hospital to this groaning world? this lazar-house of corruption and woe, that goes swinging through the ages to one unceasing anthem of pain. Men would make their fate utterly hopeless, their damnation doubly sure, could they extinguish the only light which can lead them from that doom of unrepented sin, whose horror is that it forever gathers blackness as it rolls and rolls throughout eternal night.

There are persons who judge of Christians as a man would judge of apples, who should enter an orchard and go stooping along upon the ground in search of them. He picks up one, a hard, green thing, no bigger than a walnut. He bites it; it is sour and bitter; it puckers up his mouth and sets his teeth on edge. "Ha!" he says, throwing the untimely fruit away, "I hear them speak of apples as being so delicious—I'm sure I don't think much of this one."

He picks up another which looks yellow. There's a hole in it, but he don't know what that means, so he bites into it and finds a worm.

"Bah! apples! delicious indeed!" he cries in disgust; and then picks up a third which is crushed by his touch, for it is rotten. So he condemns apples, because he has looked for them upon the ground instead of on the trees above his head, where they hang ripe, juicy, and luscious, a chief treasure of autumn.

Just so men judge of Christians so long as they take for fair samples those that lie rotten on the ground.

The young minister, having just finished his course, sometimes says, "Now here I am, poor, miserable sinner that I am, with the harvest of twenty years' study in my brain; what must I do with myself? Must all this learning, must my powers and genius be buried in some obscure hamlet? No! I must have a field worthy of my talents." And so he is found hanging about the purlieus of large towns and cities, waiting for vacancies in distinguished places. If he gets such a place as he thinks worthy of him, he soon gets a hint from his own people that he had better go down lower; and then he gets the bronchitis, or is called to a professorship, or something of that sort (for people will lie like witches about this sort of thing); and his people will endow a professorship and place their D.D. there in order to get rid of him respectably when he has used himself up on their hands.

The story that goes out to the world is: "The Rev. Dr. So-and-so was called to take a professor's seat, and has therefore resigned the charge of his people for this new, and in some respects, more important field of labor."

Now, to all in general, but to young ministers in particular, does Christ's injunction to take first the lowest seat, apply. It is sense and sound philosophy as well as proper humility to do so. The call will be "Come up higher" as soon as the man has filled and made to overflow the first place assigned him. Learn from nature how to become great and strong. Look at the acorn—it is content to go into the ground and be covered—it is content to lie long in darkness hidden away from the knowledge of all. And what then? Why then it is content to be a little germ no larger than a knitting-needle; and what then? Why then it goes on for a long time striking its roots hither and thither, grappling itself more and more firmly into the earth, working with all its strength under ground. And then? Why then it is content to be for a whole year, a single shoot no bigger than a whip; and for another year it is content to be two shoots; the third to have its shoots grow a little longer and be headed by green tips. And for ten years it grows no larger than that a man's strength can uproot it; but in fifteen or twenty years it is beyond the strength of man; and in thirty or forty years it stands aloft—a wrestler with the winds, able to take a hug with storm and winter. In fifty or a hundred years, tempests cannot upheave it from the earth; its foundations are as the rock; they cannot be shaken. Thus should it be with man. Art called to be a scullion or a street-cleaner? act well your humble part and you shall soon find yourself in one that is higher; but be sure that God will never commence for you the work of saintship where you are *not*, but where you *are*. Fill full, of yourself, the spot where God has placed you; grow daily till the place overflows with you, and your borders will surely be enlarged. So shall you rise upward, step by step, on secure footing, until at last you shall sit down in that highest of all apartments from which, since its name is heaven, none are ever ejected.

My heart is sick! I see men going to destruction on every hand, and I have no power to stay them.

What a business is that of a preacher. What a calling is that which sends one to seek men's souls even at the very gates of perdition, and often vainly—only now and then one rescued. If you could know what causes lie at the foundation of this and that sermon that I preach here, with my soul faint with yearning over this one and that in this great congregation, you would not wonder that I say I feel crushed, overborne, by the weight that is upon me.

THERE are some men who are so proud that they don't intend to enter the church until they become so good that they can confer an honor upon the church by entering it. They say, "Look out for a striking conversion, and for a high-toned, consistent Christian life, when I start. I'll set an example to those members who are such a disgrace to the church that I, sinner as I am, am ashamed of them." Ah! self-deluded man, you never will get God to dwell in your heart until it comes out of that proud frame. He don't expect you to confer honor on his church by entering it, at least not in the way you imagine. You have got to go in through the door of humility; you have got to come to that state in which you shall forget everything but that you are a lost and ruined sinner, and that your only hope, as the only hope of a murderer, is in him who will accept nothing but a broken and contrite heart. The language of a man entering the church is not, "I have become so good, that I will now join myself to the members of Christ, and thenceforth be a pattern to all who know me, and an honor to

God;" it is, "I have discovered my lost and wretched condition, and that I am too weak to stand alone. I have cast my soul upon Christ's mercy, and I beseech his children, if there is any strength or safety in the church, to take me in and watch over and help me." When you have been humbled then you may be lifted up, but "before honor goeth humility." Suppose one went to the wheat, as it waved in the field, and said: "Would you like to be made into a loaf for the queen?" "Yes," answers the wheat, "oh! yes, we should like to be presented to the queen," and on it waves, swelling with pride at the thought of its consequence. But the reaper comes, and the wheat gets a stroke at the roots and is laid prostrate. "Alas!" it sighs, "is this *going to the queen?*" But there it lies, drying in the scorching sun; and then 'tis drawn to the threshing floor, and bruised and beaten without mercy. After this 'tis winnowed, and then tied up in darkness and carried to the mill. "Is not this almost over?" cries the poor wheat, but 'tis poured into the hopper and ground to powder. Then 'tis pressed and packed, and that is not all. It is mixed with water; it is worked and kneaded; it is subjected to various rapid changes, and finally to the process of cutting and shaping into loaves. "Ah! shall I not rest now?" sighs the poor wheat. "Yes; *now* you may rest," says the baker; and forthwith shoves the loaf into a heated oven. When baked, and not till then, it is fit to be eaten; and is presented to the queen. If God intends to honor you by allowing you to honor him, he will lay you low, he will flail you, he will winnow you and grind you, he will knead and fashion you, and pass you through the fire; and then you will have discovered what it is needful to do with pride.

MEN should all have their feet on the same level, with leave to grow as high as they can from the charter God put in their souls. Oregon pines are three hundred feet high—how *solitary* their tops must be; but they start from the same place that the shrub does.

SOME men—good men after a fashion, think there is nothing in the world so hard as that they are not so high now as they have been. Their pride and their vanity suffer. What is the trouble, friend; can't you walk down there?

"Oh, yes."

"Can't you procure enough to eat?"

"Oh, yes."

"Have you not shelter?"

"Yes, I have."

"And clothes?"

"Well, yes."

"Can't you get along comfortably?"

"Yes; but then I used to live in a four-story house, and move in higher society. And my children are not where I intended that they should be," etc.

Man! are you a child of God? Have you not the inheritance of the universe by reversion? Only wait awhile. Have you not the sympathy and love of your Father, and a birth-right to eternity? What are you grumbling at? Stand upright like a man, a prince. Lift up your front and say in true manliness, "I can afford to stand in the valley. I think I could stand safely on the top of the mountain, but there are many there who could *not* afford to stand in the valley with me.

Prayer covers the whole of a man's life. There is no thought, feeling, yearning, or desire, however low, trifling, or vulgar we may deem it, which, if it affects our real interest or happiness, we may not lay before God and be sure of his sympathy. His nature is such that our often coming does not tire him. The whole burden of the whole life of every man may be rolled onto God and not weary him, though it has wearied the man.

Some may be content to regard God as a being of crystalline purity and awful majesty, to be worshipped afar off, and not troubled with the details of daily life and conflict; but others need a God to whom they can come *near*, and on whose bosom they can lean their heads, and be welcome there. They think of him nine times with a gush of filial love, where they do so once with solemn and shivering awe. They know that he loves each one of his children with a separate and peculiar love, and that he knows each one by name.

Pray out your life to God. "Be instant in prayer," and the only way to do this, is to go to him in all moods; in joy and sorrow, in depression and mirth, in hope and fear; with everything that is in you, or that touches you. Confide in God—make him your familiar friend. Keep open the path from your heart to the heart of God, and let airy feet be always treading its trackless way.

There is prayer that is too deep for words, or even groans. Have you never lain prostrate before God in the consciousness that his eye was reading all that you could not tell him?

No need to explain things to God, as one must do to the *dearest* human friend. No fear of his betraying what we pour into his ear. Come boldly and gladly to his feet; let him be to you as sunshine on the mountains, to attract and warm, rather than as the shadows of those mountains which can only awe.

The heart that cannot open to the eye of man goes naked and open into the presence of its God. There, all the sealed fountains are unclosed; there, all the secrets which must ever be secrets from the nearest and most beloved earthly friend, are disclosed, and the shrinking and sensitive soul has no reserve. Thus, we have sat down in the forest on a summer's day, and as long as men and boys tramped by, and the clatter and clash of business was heard, there was no movement in the forest; but when the din had ceased, when the footsteps had died away, and we sat motionless as the tree which supported us, there was a twitter overhead, and then an answer from another tree-top. Then out hopped a bird, and lifted up its voice in song, and then a squirrel ran along the ground, and one by one all the mysteries and confidences of the forest were revealed to us. Thus unfolds the soul of man when none but God is near; when it is hungering and thirsting after either the higher or the lower wants of life; when it is yearning for its Father, or when it is home-sick for heaven.

There be ecstacies in prayer, when the soul exults like birds on a fair morning in spring; and there be agonies of prayer, when the burden of the soul cannot be even groaned out. We must bear the burden of Christ, the burden of souls; this he permits, and when we are before God, wrestling for the brother, the child, the loved friend of whatever name, when we think of that dear soul, glowing amid everlasting light, or wailing amid everlasting shadows, *what words can ease us?*

It is not truth nor philosophy to say that prayer alters nothing, that the laws of nature are fixed, and that entreaty cannot change them. The laws of nature *are fixed on purpose to be used for the granting of prayer.* Any *man* can use the laws of nature to grant the requests of his child. Does he say that God, who made those laws, cannot do as much with them as *he* can?

Spontaneity in prayer we claim, as that which is most natural to us; but far be it from our thought to condemn form for those who can thus pray best. Let no man bind or shackle another man's conscience, or try to walk by another man's light. Let each be true to himself. Oh! let the soul alone; respect its moods and impulses. Judge not each other. Let each sinner pray as best he can, come unto God as best he may, but *let him come.*

The soul of man sways hither and thither like the sea, tossed by restless yearnings, and passions, and fears; and there is no shore against which it may break and rest, but the bosom of its God.

CHRIST spoke most to the masses clinging to the edge of life, struggling, and straining all their nerves to keep from slipping off. Their most important petition, the burden of their daily cry—"bread," "bread!" not "home," "pleasure," "children," but simply "bread."

I'VE seen luxuriant grasses growing on the tops of graves; I've seen flowers springing from the crevices of tombs; and like these are the fair and lovely moralities, and the social virtues which adorn the character of him who is not born of God's Spirit. The corpse, with its corruptions, its wasting flesh, and its decaying bones, is beneath the fragrant flowers.

To understand how the imagery of Jesus seemed to those who heard it, we should try to enter into their circumstances. To speak of the delight and refreshment of water in Great Britain, where it is almost a nuisance, would be folly. To discourse eloquently of the refreshment of the shadow of a great rock to an inhabitant of mountain gorges, where *sunshine* is the thing desirable, would be a waste of power and time.

But when we remember that in the land where

most of the Scriptures were written there was, for the greater part of the year, but burning and scorching heat; that there was *no* winter, as we understand the term; that water was as precious as gold; and that the digging of a well was the work of kings and princes; that shadow was a luxury, to attain which hours of sore and weary travelling were accounted well spent—we can better understand the beauty and force of such figures as Jesus uses in speaking to the woman of Samaria.

Digging a well rendered a man the benefactor of his race. "Canst thou do more than dig a well?" was the meaning of the woman's question to Jesus. This discourse of Jesus to her is an example of his usual mode. Never did *he* begin at abstractions, or first things. He never began by thinking away back amid mist and mystery; but from the simple, every day events of life he took his texts, and preached backward and upward to principles. In what entirely different keys were the two (Christ and the woman) conversing: This was one of those double meaning conversations that Christ delighted in. The woman and he were standing as two might stand with a wire gauze window-shade between them. He that is within the shade can see out well enough, but he that is without cannot see in. Christ was within; he saw on both sides of the curtain; but the woman stood without, darkly wondering of what water he was speaking.

MEN should not be mere indexes; not condensed and abridged editions; they should be themselves in full. Every man has a right to be all that God intended he should be, all that he has God's commission for in his own nature. And none have a right to hinder human growth. Take off the millstones; untie the bands; give man room—freedom.

COMMON things are dearer to Christ than the refined and exclusive evolvements of culture. Things common to all men are more and better in his estimation than the things that are peculiar to a class.

THE Christianity of the present age is *dead* compared with what it should be. When I lived out West our wells were all dug very shallow, and when a drought came the water failed. Then we sent a man down into the well to dig another within it, and by and by he came to water far below the first well. But if the rain was long withheld this well also failed. Then the man was sent a third time to dig and dig, until at length he struck the living springs, which flow perpetually, which no drought can affect. Many people think that after conversion religion will take care of itself. That water once gained there will always be a sufficient supply. There are whole churches whose religion is but a few feet deep. As long as showers are abundant this may do, but when they do not fall often the wells are dry. Let this not be so with you. Sink the shaft deeper and deeper still, until within you bubbles up that living water which runneth from beneath the throne of God. Don't depend on *showers* of grace. Be not at all content until the river is within your own souls.

We must either conclude that the piety of the present day is a different thing from what it was intended by Christ to be, or that he spoke the language of exaggeration. That he did *not* thus speak we know by the momentary elevations which we experience, when we rise into some nearness to the place where it is our right always to stand; and can return with rapture the smile of our Father's love. There are seasons when our souls exhale, and sit singing, like birds, in the very tree of life.

Oh! when I look upon the sun, and see what it has power to do—when I see that on the barren soil it flings a warm and radiant scarf of light, and that beneath that scarf springs up life! life! life! and gorgeous beauty, and lavish and redolent bloom, I know that the Sun of Righteousness has a greater power than this, if men's stiff, and frozen and faithless hearts will but open themselves to his rays.

The love of God! who can fathom it? We soon cloy with honey; 'tis not very hard to satisfy ourselves with sugar; even of bread we may tire; but who ever tired of air? All day we breathe it; at morning, at noon, at night, all night—all our lives, and we are not weary. *Love* is the *vital air* of the soul.

Every earthly pleasure wearies, but of spiritual pleasures we never tire. The more we are filled with them the more hungry and thirsty after them we grow; and we are more sure, the more we taste the love of God, that it can fill us, and be always about us, and be always peace and everlasting joy.

Why do we not bud and bloom more gloriously beneath the shining of this sun of love?

It is because we have portioned him, we have limited him, we have not consecrated to him the whole of our lives. We give him our Sabbaths, our morning and our evening hours of prayer, our feelings of solemnity and self-condemnation, our hours of depression and tears; we go to him in trouble, and gloom, and fear, we call upon him early when all is dark about us; but from our business, from our pleasure, from our social and common life, we put him away. Our brightest and most agreeable, and our busiest and most useful hours we keep for ourselves and our fellows; but we go with our unhappy and unattractive moods and feelings, with long, forlorn faces, and tearful eyes, to wait upon our God. Can this be well-pleasing in his sight? If a lover or a bridegroom gave his chosen fair a diamond to wear upon her breast, and she should wear it joyfully at all times, save when she came into his presence, and then should carefully hide it from sight, would he not have a right to complain? but what diamond ever sparkled with so radiant a light as shines a smile upon the human face, and when it is a heart-smile, it hath a priceless value. God gave man power to smile—and man only, of all creatures, possesses that power—why should he seek to hide his smiles and innocent mirth from him who made and loves them?

Did Christ keep his religion for the pulpit, and fear to "degrade his office" by mixing with and trying to influence the masses? Did he attempt to keep his disciples unspotted from the world by shutting them from the rush and turmoil of the world?

Consecrating your life to Christ is not giving up all the pleasures and beauties of life. Take all of these that he gives you, and use them gladly and gratefully, as gifts from him, to be resigned if he so wills it. Be as joyful, as happy—aye, as *merry* as you will, while the sunshine is upon you, but when the shadows fall be patient; and be filled alway with abundant love for him. Let that love for him go into every act of your life, whether civil or religious. Make every act a religious act.

When Christians learn to do *all things* as unto Christ, then will the church arise and her light come; *but* while religion and ministers are kept pretty much confined to the pulpit, the prayer-meeting, the study, and the family altar, darkness will be on souls and over the earth.

There are two great difficulties in presenting this subject. One is that you all know so little about it; *the other* is, that *I* know so little about it. We have become so accustomed to the *cant* of piety —so satisfied with a heavy heart, and a solemn face, so used to pray and pray, and then go away and forget that every act should be as a prayer; that, say what we may, we hardly realize that love to God should be *love,* or that his love to us *is* actual love—a passion, warmer than ever swells in human breast—real, throbbing, yearning love, that knows us each by name, and longs to have us allow him to fit us for that larger life where all that is here denied to us shall be freely given.

For in heaven the good things that we have now but in part shall be perfected; and every single pure yearning of our nature shall be abundantly fulfilled.

Here we are like plants which the gardener keeps in pots till they are ready to be transplanted. Often we are in every way very much cramped while here; there we shall have root room, and branch room, and the promise of our nature shall be more than made good. We shall be made all glorious, and be satisfied with our inheritance.

God does not mock us. He plants no yearning in the human soul which he does not intend to satisfy; he gave no capacity which he does not intend shall find scope for everlasting accomplishment.

I apprehend that the words of Scripture are often more literal than we suppose. The Christian really has truer possession of the things that now are, as well as ownership of the things that are to come.

Alas! for the sorrowful, the lonely, and the hopeless, that refuse their rightful inheritance!

The difference in the life of a believer and in that of an unbeliever is the difference of eternity.

The latter plans for a few years, eighty at most. He says, "My faculties will improve for so long, and then decay; my genius will lighten for so long, and then grow dim; my friends are my friends while I live; my children I love for all this life." The whole range of his thought of living is within a hundred years.

But the Christian says, "My faculties may fail because of the failing of flesh; but they will rally, and open, and grow forever. I am not improving myself for a few years' use, but for eternal ages. If my genius slumbers here, it will awake yonder, beyond the stars, and sparkle in the brightness of God's glory. My friends, familiar and dear, are to be mine, and our love is to strengthen and deepen forever. My children! the grave *may* hide them, but only for a moment; they are *mine*, for the cycles of eternity. Yea, and all that is in the universe is mine, and God is mine, and I am his forever."

THE man who knows he has but one talent feels easier about improving it than he can who is conscious of possessing many.

The more a man rises the more earnest is he to do the work which he was sent to do. Life seems short and every step of it *full* of his destiny. *No man can do the work of any other man.*

To persons sincerely anxious to leave the world wiser and better than they found it, but who feel as if they were as yet almost useless in their generation, let this thought give consolation. Many persons live out half their lives, some even three-quarters, before they come to the peculiar work which they were sent to do. Meantime they are doing good by shedding a right influence.

The mourner over a wasted life may yet be shown that he was fruitful of good when he knew it not. From him there may be going sweet influences like the fragrance of flowers.

Some people blossom almost as soon as they enter life, and then they depart. The flower that opens when it first breaks from the ground, and then dies, is an emblem of our infants that die. Violets are the children and youth who finish their mission near life's entrance, and then depart. We mourn for them, and say: "How mysterious! cut off when so full of promise!" but we *should* congratulate them.

Then there are June flowers, and flowers that do not blossom till July or August. These latter, and the strong September flowers, go all the spring time, and for months after, gathering strength for final putting forth. Their time has not been wasted; though to the eyes of those who know them not they have seemed but idle, homely things.

When they do put forth they hold on bravely till the frost kills leaf and flower.

Let not that man think his life wasted who can go home to heaven bearing blossoms, though *late* blossoms, on every limb.

There is something beautiful to me in the thought that there is a specialty of work for each man.

In work, as in character, disposition, history and destiny, there is a specialty; and when the church arises to the New Jerusalem it will not be to sit there as one vast photographic likeness, nor shall one be able to say of its members, "I have heard their history," when the story of ONE has been told.

The history of the church will be made up of individual histories; and each one shall possess its own peculiar interest.

Your history will be none the less interesting when *mine* has been told, nor mine when you have related yours. Your head and heart will not be as mine, nor mine as yours; we shall not be mere fragments of a universal church; but we shall be fully, roundly, and conspicuously ourselves, *in* the church of which we make a whole, and perfect, and unexampled individual.

WE regret that all Christ's words were not saved, even though they multiplied books as John supposes they would. Yet we already have more than we heed; and necessity demands no more, though curiosity does. When I remember how closely that rough, knotty, gnarled old Johnson was followed, and every word from his lips treasured up; when I think how the words of that incarnation of refined selfishness, Goethe, were saved, I cannot but say in my heart: Why was there no such record kept of the sayings of the man Christ Jesus?

WHAT labor seems too hard when it is done for love? I don't think it would be very easy to induce me to become a basket-maker; *but* were it by that trade alone that I could hope to gain some maiden whom I loved, *I would like to see the man who would sing more than I would over his weaving.* Now to you whose lot in life is cast in some uncongenial field, whose labor is with distaste and heaviness of heart, Christ says: "Do it as if for *me.* I'll be your lover. Work where vou are for me, and my love shall reward you."

THE heart of woman yearns for love more than for any other thing, and when she asks it of God, he replies: "Certainly, my child, if you can bear all that goes with love." But if God loves her, and sees that she is asking what will do her harm, he will not grant her prayer.

The man that prays for wealth may have it, if he is able to bear the discipline necessary to prevent it from proving his ruin.

One who is bound for destruction may escape the stripes that will fall upon the *Christian's* back who attempts to set his heart on mortal lover, or on uncertain riches.

They who make gods of goods, and go bowed down under the gold they carry, are worse off than they are who journey wearily over the hot sands of the desert. For the pilgrims have camels to bear *their* burdens, while they who trust in riches are their own beasts of burden. They crouch down and cry, "More, pile on more," and more is often given them; for if a man *will* have his portion on earth it is sometimes given him, and so he goes toiling beneath his load, with gold on his back, and hell in his heart, down to destruction.

It has ever been a mystery to the so-called Liberals, that the Calvinists, with what they have considered their harshly despotic and rigid views and doctrines, should always have been the staunchest and bravest defenders of freedom. The working for Liberty of these severe principles in the minds of those that adopted them has been a puzzle. But the truth lies here—Calvinism has done what no other religion has ever been able to do. It presents the highest human ideal to the world, and sweeps the whole road to destruction with the most appalling battery that can be imagined. It intensifies, beyond all example, the individuality of man, and shows in a clear and overpowering light his responsibility to God, and his relations to eternity. It points out man as entering life under the weight of a tremendous responsibility; having, on his march towards the grave, this *one sole chance* of securing heaven and of escaping hell.

Thus the Calvinist sees him pressed, burdened, urged on, by the most mighty influencing forces. He is on the march for eternity; and is soon to stand crowned in heaven, or to lie sweltering in hell, thus to continue forever and ever.

Who shall *dare* to fetter such a being? Get out of his way! Hinder him not! or do it at the peril of your own soul. Leave him *free* to find his way to God. Meddle not with him or with his rights. Let him work out his salvation as he can. No hand must be laid crushingly upon a creature who is on such a race as this. A race whose end is to be eternal glory, or unutterable woe forever and forever.

They tell us that Calvinism plies men with hammer and with chisel. It *does;* and the result is the monumental marble.

Other systems leave men soft and dirty. Calvinism makes them of white marble to endure forever.

You all hate tyrants; but not half so much as God hates a slave. Not that he does not pity the poor slave; but when he looks on him he says, "*This* is not *my* work. I never made this. This is not what I intended when I made a man. I made him in my image, to stand royally before me, to be united to me by loyal love, not to become a creature like this."

When a man says to me, "When I saw that mother weeping, and her house burning, and when I rushed into the flames, and at the peril of my own life saved and restored to her her child, am I to be told that *that* was not a good action—that it was a sin in the sight of God?"

Not by me, friend, not by me. That *was* a good action. It was a hint of what there is planted in your nature by God; and it shows your guilt in not coming to the Sun of Righteousness, that all such things within you may be warmed into a continual life.

A man who is capable of such generous acts ought to be ashamed not to be what the love of God would make him. And if he will not love God, and be made into his image, he needs *no other* condemnation. It is not by the fits and starts of your conduct that you are to be judged, but by its *whole course.* And if the centre and ruling principle of your life be not love to God, you are radically and fatally wrong.

When we tell you that you are without God, you run and gather up all your occasional emotions of gratitude towards him, and of admiration for him, and heaping them together before us, say, "What! *I* without God!"

Now, you may feel admiration, even very warm admiration, for God—every refined and thoughtful mind must; and perhaps, when you are on the summit of your joys, just as you cross the highest line, you look off, and say, "Thank God! thank God!" it may be very heartily; but does your gratitude and love for him go down beneath thought and feeling, and take hold upon the secret springs of your soul? Is your life directed, ruled, and formed by that love? Can you look upward and say, with glowing breast, "Father, Abba, Father!"

If not, your love is but the starlight, and the moonlight, when it should be the light of the fervid sun.

Why, when the sun shines with long, slant ray, on Greenland, what lives or thrives beneath its power? But when he pours down straight from his meridian, there springs up life and luxuriant growth.

Such love as you speak of is the slant beam of the winter sun, or like the shining of moonbeams on Nova Zembla.

You cannot go to heaven with *that* love. You must be born again. Your *course* must be changed.

Why, suppose a shipmaster starts from New York harbor for the Mediterranean Sea. He goes beautifully out of the harbor, and steers straight for Greenland. Off Newfoundland he is hailed by another sail. His destination is inquired and given.

"Bound for Malta!" shouts the stranger. "You? Why, you're steering for the North Pole."

"Don't tell me *that*," returns our captain, very much offended—"Don't tell me that. My ship is good and well stored; my men are good, and they find me the most generous of captains. They have long sleeping hours and short watches; they have abundance of all that is good for food. In my cabin are plenty of books and flowers, and we have fine times down there. We enjoy ourselves very much indeed—don't tell me that all this time we are on our way to any place but Malta; I don't believe it."

The stranger passes on, saying derisively: "I

don't care how good you are to your men, or how many good books or beautiful flowers you have got below; all this is very fine, no doubt; but I say that the man that's going to Malta, and heading direct for the North Pole, is *a fool.*" And so he is; all his flowers won't save him. His *course* must be changed; and it's just so about the sinner. He's heading for hell; and all the flowers and all the good things that are in him won't save him, if he don't *turn short about.* He is living for self when he should be living for God. Self is his idol, when he should worship God. He is all wrong, wrong, and will certainly be lost if he doesn't come to Jesus for help, safety, and grace to fit him for heaven.

"But," do you say: "must a man be converted when he is already good enough?"

Certainly not. If he is as good as conversion can make him, he may go to heaven on that ground; there is no jealousy in the matter. If you can *deserve* heaven, God is perfectly willing that you should do so.

If any of you can go to him and say truly, "Lord, I've always loved thee with all my heart, and strength, and mind, and my neighbor as myself—need I be converted? Can't I go to heaven as I am?" God will answer:

"Yes, certainly, you are like the angels, and need no conversion or redemption."

Now I would like to see *all in this congregation who feel as though they could honestly say this to God, rise up where they are. I would like to count them.* What! not one? Is there not *one* in this great congregation who dare make such a plea? Then you have no plea that will stand you for a moment.

Suppose that some provision for all your past sins could be made, and you started to-morrow morning to begin life anew. You say to pride: "Now, pride, you're not going to be master any more. I'm going to be master now; I'll hold you in; I'll tread on you." And you go forth and return at night lamenting thus: "Pride has overcome me, and ran away with me; it has dashed me almost to atoms; I cannot stand at all against its diabolical power."

Then you say to your other passions, "Lie down, I *will* be master;" and they rise up and roar at you; they wrestle with and cast you down; they rend and worry you, leaving you nigh to death. *Then* you begin to see *what* you are and *where* you are, and you bemoan yourself thus: "I never was half so bad as this till I tried to grow better. I had not a thought of the strength of the evil nature in me; I *cannot* reform. Oh! wretched man that I am, *who* shall deliver me from the body of this death." *Now* you are in the right place to hear that Jesus Christ will deliver you. His power can convert you, and will do it if you are in earnest in asking. And then *he* will take care of your sins; all you will have to do will be to forget them. Go heartily to work for him; work for him in your own heart, for you will always find plenty to do there; and work for him in the world, in your business, your studies, your pleasure, your *whole* life, work for him. Your most radical and central ideas must be Godward before you will be headed right and sailing heavenward. Beware! if a slow-match be placed by the magazine, you may heap the building with gardens full of flowers, but they will not save you from being blown sky-high when the fire reaches the powder.

Oh! men! men! men! struck through with the rottenness of sin, come out of the darkness, escape for your lives. Ye young, come to the light, come to joy, come to immortal life.

If all unkind and unjust words were arrows, like needles and pins; and if, instead of piercing the ear and then the heart, they flew against the bodies of those to whom they were directed, the children in some men's families would be like pin-cushions stuck completely full of sharp and painful weapons.

THE command of Christ to take up the cross has been signally and widely misunderstood. The Christian life presents so broad a front, that all views blend in it. *This* is but *one*. They err who would make it *the* characteristic of religion.

Deny thyself, and take thy cross; but still be not seeking for burdens. If the Lord says to thee, "Go forward," *go*, though the next step be over a precipice five hundred feet deep, where far below you trees look like grass. The air may become solid beneath your feet; but if not, *go forward* where duty calls, and *the end* shall be peace and life; but don't be ever feeling as if the burden of the Lord was heavy, and to be borne with groans, and bent frame, and sighings—or that you must turn from life's pleasures, merely because they *are* pleasures, and it would be denying yourself to forsake them.

Christianity asks no such sacrifices. She gives *fullness* to the joys of life, saying only, walk in the love and fear of God; rejoice freely in all life's pure pleasures, but murmur not if God see fit to take them from you. Be patient when the trial comes, but be not seeking poverty of any earthly delight.

Not such jesuitical notions are those of Christianity. Men are not called upon to empty themselves of the loves of earth, and to become ghostly, and ghastly despisers of its warmth and beauty.

They are called to bring all that is natural within them, given of God in the beginning, and have it sanctified, then love shall tell them where to take up the cross, and where to deny themselves; and soon there will be only strength in the cross, and choice in the self-denial; for as the higher faculties grow and rise, the lower will cause less and less pain in submitting. They will mind quickly, at the first start of their superiors, and what *was* sore self-denial will be so no longer.

The time when Christians will be no longer called to poverty and hardness, to narrowness and commonness of outward life, is coming. We are on the edges of it, and therefore I speak to warn you to consecrate your prosperity and your pleasures to the Lord. The earth is the Lord's, and the fullness thereof; and all that is rich, and tasteful, and beautiful, he will give into the hands of his own children. The devil has stolen the wealth and beauty of this world; but he cannot retain it. All that taste and riches can command is yet to be bestowed upon the church; when she shall have become so pure that she can stand blameless, generous, honest, and humble, in prosperity and luxury. Christians have yet to learn—and they *will* learn it—the lesson of humility and godliness in the midst of riches.

They will learn how to walk aright not in sackcloth, but in velvet; how to be not only steadfast under affliction, but under blessing. They will be able to endure not only hardness, but what is far more dangerous, *softness*—and will be able to bear not only defeat and baffling, but *victory*.

I WISH that I could see a right sort of prayer-meeting. We have better prayer-meetings here than they do in many places; but I have heard in this lecture-room prayers that I don't think went higher than the ceiling, and talks that had no life in them, said simply because you had come to say something, and thought that was about the right thing to say.

Now if I could hear a man standing up in his place, say,

"I'm cross at home. I trouble my wife. I am harsh and ungentle to my children. I don't represent to them at all the character of God. Indeed, I'm afraid if God were presented to them as their *father*, that they would be more inclined to run away from him than if they viewed him solely as a judge. My brethren, I don't want to be such a wicked Christian. I am sorry and sad because I am such. Can you tell me how to improve?"

Or: "Brethren, I'm stingy—dreadful stingy and

harsh. I do give sometimes; but it comes very hard. I want to get as much work out of everybody as I can for the least pay. I try to be prudent by getting good bargains out of other people. When I can buy a good garment at half price, or when I can get a day's work out of a poor person for half a day's wages, I generally do it. Can any of you show me how to get a generous heart?"

Or: "I'm growing rich, and I feel the swellings of vanity and self-importance already beginning in my heart. Can you tell me how to keep humble, and to glorify God in what I keep for myself, as well as in what I give away?"

Then I should say we are having a genuine work of grace in our meeting. My people, we must make our religion fit *our* times, *our* dispositions, and *our* wants, and not try to torture ourselves into the shapes of ancient times. The first Christians were forced to apply religion chiefly to supporting themselves under losses, privations, and persecutions; but we need to apply it more in other directions. Our tempers, our households, our business, our political duties, our pecuniary circumstances, must all be guided by religion, or we are faithless in our generation.

I don't know which is most lovely and admirable, a poor and devoted saint at the very gate of starvation, who is full of love and grace, and who is ever doing good, or a rich and lifted up saint, who, with not a want that need go ungratified, who is yet as pure and humble, as self-denying and generous as though he had never known wealth. But the latter needs most grace to keep him.

THE world is God's journal wherein he writes his thoughts, and traces his tastes. The world overflows with beauty. Beauty should no more be called trivial, since it is the thought of God. Through beauty things become useful. It is a religious duty for a man, so far as honestly he can, to surround his children with creations of taste and beauty, that their finer instincts may be cultured and gratified. The love of beauty is the gift of God, and it is born in the heart of every child.

MANY good people think it wrong to indulge in a taste for the fine arts. They are even much exercised by conscience for wearing expensive clothing. They lay off broadcloth and silks, and dress in linsey-woolsey; but they may then still retrench and retrench, that they may have more for the poor; for this principle, carried out, would lead back to barbarism. It is not the right one. Every man should do his part for the poor, *and his heart should enlarge as his means increase;* but he who can earn them has a right to refinements for himself and for his children.

Men have got to learn how to unite the elegances of high polish and luxury with self-denying humility and generosity; they have got to learn how to revel amid the delights of music, poetry and painting, and not be hurt by any or all of these before the millennium will be fully established; for God's children are to walk amid all the good and beautiful things of the earth, and be holy there. No man has any business to be unrefined, or neglectful of the cultivation of taste. By the love of nature; by music and poetry, and painting; by flowers, and by the neatness and elegance of household appliances, grossness will be destroyed. It is a mark of a sinking nature to be indifferent to everything but food, clothing and shelter. Beauty in the house, beauty on the person, beauty all around, should be a man's aim; and every home should resound with melody, and be bright with the results of genius and taste—thus will be the homes of the latter day.

It is more worthy of a Christian man to take gladly and gratefully all these delights, and to learn to carry himself aright in the use of them, than it is to refuse them all, and go stinted and starved of beauty, through the world.

Accustom your children to the elegancies, refinements and beauties of life, while at the same time you train them robustly in the exercise of all that is good within them. Thus they shall grow up around you elegant, refined, beautiful; and as *agreeably*, as they are *thoroughly*, good; which will be a *very great* advantage that they will have over some of the good people of the present day, who are the most disagreeable people on earth.

Clothes and manners don't make the man; but when he *is* made, they improve his appearance.

THE sweetest and most generous natures are the ones in greatest danger of becoming soured through the ingratitude of the world.

THE family is the first, and by far the most important, institution in the world. It is the true church; the best expounder of the truths of Christianity. It is from the family that the only real idea of the relationship between God and man can be obtained; for God is more a father than he is a king, or a judge; and thus men should be taught to regard him. Paternity is the strangest of life's mysteries, and the most solemn men come here to watch that the priest teach his church right things. Look at home, father priest, mother priest, *your* church is a hundredfold heavier responsibility than mine can be. Your priesthood is from God's own hands, and it is a solemn thing to have God lay his hands upon you in paternity—to give you a church from your own loins. You should all condemn the man who should rush with haste and levity into the ministry; but not half so worthy of condemnation would he be, as they are who enter thoughtlessly, led but by fancy and youthful inclination, into the marriage state, and are constituted priests of the family. They are the formers of immortal characters as no other priests can ever be. Let them look well to *how* they form them.

Children are not given primarily for your love, or for your amusement, though incidentally they are for these; nor are they given for a staff for your old age, though they shall be this also, if you are the wise support of their youth; but they are given for your education, and to become, like you, independent beings.

You are not to consider them as burdens, or to repine that you are wearing out your life for them, but you are to guide them carefully; to instruct them fully in the path by which they are to journey when they may no longer cling to your hand. Teach them so that when you leave them to go on alone, they may know how to steer for the safe haven. If you do your duty faithfully, you will reap your reward as you go along; if you fail, *bitter* will be your punishment; for no keener suffering can be known on earth, than that which the heart of a parent bleeds under when the hand that administers it is the hand of his own child.

A man who has never had the care nor felt the love of little children, who has not been taught self-denial by his desire for their good, is, so far forth, not a perfect man.

I do not say that the discipline must of necessity come through children of his own blood; but he must be taught of childhood, or he is forever unfinished.

FOR a poisoned heart there is nothing in the world so poisonous as men. It is not *well* to see *too much* of men.

I CAN conceive of a state of public sentiment and morals, in which there might properly be free utterance of truths, which in the present state of society a minister has not a right to express.

The people could not understand or bear them now, and to speak them out would be to touch morality, and to cause great evil. This, in the days of Christ and his apostles, was the case in regard to many truths which it is now the leading duty of his ministers to proclaim boldly. As the ages pass, the circumstances of men change, and truth must be brought to bear on men as they can bear it. Premature developments work mischief. This principle both Christ and his disciples fully recognized, and *many yet* are the secret truths of God. The future will unfold them as they are needed.

When sick of humanity, away to the desert, the forest, or the ocean shore; there is balm in nature for the wounded and weary heart; healing is in all her low uttered voices.

Men who were to treat their social affections as we treat our religious ones, would be regarded as fools—and with reason. While we are busied with the pressing affairs of life, we *cannot* feel the glow of religious affection—nor is it expected. If, when the pauses of business come (not when we pause from exhaustion, but in the leisure hours)—our soul gladly returns unto its love; or if, when in the hurry of work and trade, a question of *principle* comes up, our thoughts glance quickly Godward, *and we decide as in his presence*, we need not fear that we are in a cold, back-slidden state, though we be, indeed, *very* diligent in business. To have the fear of the Lord always before one, it is *not* necessary that one should be always directly thinking of him, or of spiritual things. This is impossible in those pauses of daily life, where it is our *duty* to concentrate thought upon secular concerns. "Ye cannot serve God and mammon," has been perverted to mean that it was unchristian for a man ever to give his whole attention to money making.

Now the whole attention of a man must be given to study, during study hours, or he will never make a scholar; and it must be equally given to business, during business hours, or he will never succeed in the proper support of his family, or the Gospel. When the work and the strain is over, *then* the soul of the Christian will consciously rejoice in the Lord.

What if I, on awaking, were to say: "Now, I will love my family with all my heart—nothing shall, this day, interfere with my love for them," and were then to go into a furious fervor about it, embracing and kissing them, and declaring my affection for them. I might *try* to work, with my mind so hotly fixed on them, but I could not do it. I should soon say: "I can't hunt up these texts—I can't write these sermons—they require my whole attention, and that is not justice to my wife and children—they turn away my thoughts and affections from my family—I will no longer try to work at them." I then impatiently toss books and papers aside, and devoting myself to the declarative form of love for my family, forget all else. How much good should I do them under such circumstances? The true way to prove my love for them is, to devote myself steadily to some way of supporting them. Then, at the season of relaxation from work, I shall be sure to enjoy them and their love.

Just so in spiritual matters; for the family is the best teacher of theology. The men who walk in lonely places, thinking only of God and the angels, are not the most reliable Christians—are not the bone and sinew of the church. This has been proved throughout the ages.

Any such thought of the things unseen and eternal, as shall unfit a man for his daily secular duties, or teach him to despise them, is *wrong* thought, and should be discarded. Religion underlies all things. It is intended to fit a man for *life*—to teach him how to carry himself in his business, his pleasures, and his pains, as much as to aid him when he dies. It was not meant to lift him out of, or beyond, the common work or wants of life, *until life is passed.*

THE frozen ship which, last week, came struggling towards New York harbor, is a figure of man's soul before grace enters it.

Look at her condition! Her ropes and rigging incased in shining ice; her men mailed in ice—ice in their hair, ice on their beards, their feet and legs clad in the frozen mail, the gauntlets on their hands heavy and stiff with the same cold armor, and their hearts freezing in them from long struggling and despair. The pumps must be worked incessantly, to keep the ice-loaded ship afloat; but the strokes fall slower and slower, for the life is congealing in the arms of the hopeless mariners.

Hark! a hail. See! a pilot-boat is near. Another moment, and the pilot is on board.

"Give me the helm," he says to the worn-out man at the wheel. "I know just where you are, and will get you safe into port in a few hours."

The men find themselves suddenly endowed with new powers of motion. They rush about the decks, obeying the pilot's orders. They pull at the ropes; they rattle the icy shrouds, they make the crust fly from the tackling. Up the slippery ratlines they climb; they dash from the frozen rigging masses which before they could not move. The cordage creaks and groans, and its shivered mail rattles down upon the decks; sails are reefed and unreefed, they hoist this sheet, and take in that, all with the same stiff and frozen hands and limbs which, an hour before, were yielding to the torpor of death.

Cheerfulness is on all faces, hope in every heart. They have got a pilot. He will guide them into port. Their lives are saved.

The soul is that ice-bound vessel; its unrenewed powers are those ice-clad, helpless men. Grace is the pilot, whose coming renews the life and hope of all.

And grace alone can encourage one who has once seen himself to be in the wretched condition which has been described. Grace can strengthen and cheer; it can guide the soul into the safe haven. Without it there is no true life—only frost and ice, and hopeless and heavy gloom, ending in eternal death.

I WOULD pave hell with doubts; yea, I would so fill and choke it up with doubts that it could contain nothing else, could I by that undo the reality of it, and necessity for it.

HOURS are like sponges—they wipe out good resolutions.

No man ever becomes a Christian by beginning with his outward life. Reformation is not religion; though it often precedes, and always accompanies it. He who is constantly laboring to reform his conduct, and to square his life by the rules of morality while his heart is not right with God, has all the burden and cross of religion, but none of its peace.

And he will never gain much upon the work he is trying to do; for, if the very faults, from which he has for a time escaped, do not overtake him, others, perhaps worse, will, as long as the principle within him remains unchanged. He may, with strong hand and iron will, curb the outgoings of pride and passion in some old direction, but they will find new courses. There is no curing effects until causes are reached.

Camping down upon the edges of a sin from which a man has just escaped, is dangerous work. A person in such a position is like one who, upon finding himself in the running current of a river which is rising, swollen by heavy rains, struggles desperately until he reaches its banks, and there settles himself in false security. In the morning, the waters of the freshet are booming about him, and he flies to the meadow, a little higher. But the floods are out, and they rise and rise, faster than he can run, and the man who, by fleeing at once *to the mountains*, when he came up from the river, would have been saved, by tarrying upon the lowlands, perishes.

NEVER was there such a contrast in a conversation as that presented in the conversation between Christ and the woman of Samaria. Christ speaking from the top of all spiritual apprehension, the woman from the bottom of sensuous knowledge.

IN the higher sense, there is no right action without right motive, and the only right motive is, *Love to God.*

You may spend your whole life picking off your old dried leaves and dead branches, but if in the centre springs of your soul you are not subdued to God, your work, although rewarded in this life, as all morality is, will not be accepted in heaven.

I have seen a gardener at work upon a tree which had a worm gnawing into it at the point where the root and the trunk united. The earth hid the worm, and so, when the leaves withered, the owner went and picked them off, and washed the tree with the various things that he had heard recommended for diseased trees.

When the branches began to perish he hewed them off, and he worked and worked all summer at that tree, but it died. Now, had the gardener called for a spade, and removed the earth about the roots, *and killed that worm*, he might have given himself no farther trouble about the withered leaves, or the dying branches. There would have been no more of them.

The reason why inquirers cannot find the peace for which they seek, is because there is self-will hiding somewhere out of sight; like the main-spring of a watch, which cannot be seen, and which yet is the very life of motion in the watch, self-will is the ruling power in every sinner's heart. It lurks in such darkness that the man himself cannot always see it. But often he knows very well where it is snugged away; and when conviction comes upon him, when he longs to be religious and at peace, he goes with a candle into every place where this rebel is not, to hunt him out and make him surrender to God. Into all the chambers of his soul he goes with his candle. He sees how sinful he is in them, and he freely opens them to God's cleansing. He *never* set much store by anything in these rooms; but there is a dark, close closet in the mansion, from which the sinner keeps carefully away. He don't thrust his candle in *there*, and say to the thing that cowers within, "There you are; come out and be made captive." Oh! no. This is the worm at the core; and you may go on with your hard working out your salvation till you die; and if you do not unearth him, you will land in perdition.

This enemy will lurk in a closet only while he is hunted for. A culprit is hid in a house; the officers come to seek for him; the master of the mansion shows them hither and thither, bids them open this door, and that; go up garret, and down cellar, and be satisfied. But when they pass a panel in which there is a secret spring, he says not a word about it; and it remains untouched.

The officers are satisfied that the man they seek is not there, and they depart. When the door shuts behind them, the panel opens, and a face is seen at the window watching them away.

Now the culprit is out. He walks about the parlors, the halls, the chambers, just as he was wont, until there is a sound as of returning footsteps; when he instantly vanishes behind the closing panel.

Thus difficult to discover is the hiding-place of self-will. When once that principle *is* reached and grasped, the whole man can be easily guided. He *is* guided whithersoever that subtile principle wills that he should go.

Look at that stately ship. What a mighty hull she has—three hundred feet long; her masts a hundred feet high. How well set is her rigging, how clearly defined her spars. We may see her distinctly, but not *all.* Away down under the water, hiding at the ship's stern, there is a little plank that is of more importance than all that so proudly towers on the breast of the billows.

Neither hull, nor decks, nor main-mast, nor mizzen-mast, nor bowsprit, nor yards, nor sails, would be of any use without that plank down under water. Suppose that some person, ignorant of this fact, should attempt to guide that ship's course. He would say, in despair, after wearing himself out with fruitless efforts: "What *does* ail this ship? I have pulled at her bows; I have furled and unfurled her sails; I have tugged at every rope in her, but she will not keep her course. I cannot manage her. She will do nothing right. What can it mean?"

Now, suppose an old salt should say, "Have you tried the wheel?"

"Wheel?" says the man, "what wheel? No; I've tried no wheel."

"Lay hold here, my hearty," cries the sailor. The landsman grasps the wheel, and the little plank below turns two inches, and the ship, though she be ten times as large, and ten times as heavily laden, moves submissively round to the strength of one man's hand.

Now you may tug at your topmasts, or toil at your bows, and you will *die* with your course all wrong. You never will head for the safe harbor till you take your stand at the wheel.

NEVER think that God is going to make a Christian out of you without effort of your own. When the lion crouches down before you, and his eyes glare upon you, and he is about to spring, you need not expect Providence to fire your gun for you; you must do it yourself or die. 'Tis kill or be killed with you then. God has already done his part in the work of your salvation. If you don't choose to do your part you will perish.

THE moralist says, "It has cost me severe labor to be as good as I am; how shall I ever be able to do greater things than these?" Friend, there is a rock which on one side is supported by the solid earth, on another side by other rocks, on a third by trees, but upon the fourth side it has no support, and it requires there but a few pounds' weight to tip it downward.

Now you may go and destroy yourself in efforts

to remove that rock, and only imbed it deeper in the earth, or fasten it more firmly in the trees or among other rocks; but, push it *in the right direction*, and it is no longer there. I tell you it would not be half so hard to be a great deal better Christian, than to be the moralist you are. You are all the time pushing the rock the wrong way. Do you say: "Well, it is the most earnest desire of my life to become a Christian. What lack I yet? What is in the way?" I cannot tell—I might tell, in particular cases, but not generally. But, 'tis a question that each one can answer for himself, if he *is sincere* in wishing to know.

God will answer all prayer for help in such cases, when it is patiently and honestly continued.

The law is a battery which protects all that is behind it, but sweeps with destruction all that is before. Repenting toward the law is repenting toward destruction, but repenting toward God is repenting toward life and peace.

We count it marvellous that Christ bore our sins a few hours for us. Ah! God bore them long before—he bears them yet. The agony upon the cross was but one outshining upon us of his unutterable pity and love. 'Tis not at cold, bloodless, senseless law, that we strike by sin; but straight home upon the throbbing, yearning heart of God, our Father.

The world has an ugly way of forgiving. It *can* forgive; but as to *forgetting*, that's quite another thing; and it must give the offender its mind. It sets him down before the blowpipe of its indignation, and scorches him through and through. Now that is not the way that God forgives—he runs to meet a penitent while he is yet a great way off. *Runs* is the figure—not waits, not walks—*runs;* and he don't tell the trembling sinner what he thinks of him; he don't excoriate, bruise, and taunt, as the world does, till the penitent wishes a hundred times that he never had repented; but—as he himself declares—he forgives with no upbraiding; and the transgressions of the sinner shall not be even *mentioned* to him, or *remembered* against him, any more.

There are sitting before me, in this congregation, now two hundred men who stuff their Sundays full of what they call religion, and then go out on Mondays to catch their brothers by the throat, saying: "Pay me that thou owest; it's Monday now, and you needn't think that because we sat crying together yesterday over our Saviour's sufferings and love, that I'm going to let you off from that debt, if it *does* ruin you to pay it now."

Fear, in its normal action, leads towards hope. In its place it is good; but when you find that it leads to despondency, be sure that 'tis out of its place, and acting morbidly. Water is good to float timber, but a water-logged tree will certainly sink. Don't allow yourself to be water-logged by fear or anxiety.

Bad men may keep up long, but when once they fall they cannot rise again. They are like apples I have seen hanging from a tree, round and fair as they could be, but also inside as rotten as they could be. As long as they could swing upon their stem they did well enough, but when they had fallen and smashed upon the ground, I never heard of their being made good apples of afterwards.

A man who makes calculation and provision for this life only, is like a sea captain who, starting on a voyage to Europe, lays in provisions sufficient to last him only until he gets safe past the lighthouse, and out into the open sea.

There are some men's souls that are so thin, so almost destitute of what is the true idea of *soul*, that were not the guardian angels so keen-sighted they would altogether overlook them.

Men are differently built. There are men who are broad and strong at the base, in the middle, and up until you reach the moral faculties. These are shrunken in, and almost vanished.

Such men are like lighthouses, built well at the bottom, and all the way up. All right, *only* they have no lantern, and no light. And the two things, the man and the house, are equally valuable.

Each one is at liberty to fashion God so that his thought can clasp him; else there can be no *love* to God. Make him to suit your want, and you will have gratitude and love to him.

Some people, when they think of God, have a vague idea of greatness—and when they pray, they pray into nothing, hoping that, perchance, some good angel will gather up their prayers, and bear them into the divine presence.

All truth is equilibrated. Pushing any truth out very far, you are met by a counter truth. A man generally runs one truth out till he meets another, and then he drops his first truth and goes over to its counter. By and by he swings back and gains his true position, that of a hub in a wheel, with all truth pointing towards him, and meeting where he stands.

The truth of man's freedom, carried to a certain extent, is met by his dependence upon, and action according to, the will of God. The truth of a man's individuality meets, at a certain point, the truth of his sociality of being. These things are all true, and to be *right*, a man must be *on both sides.*

THE idea of right living seems to be, with some men, *not doing anything wrong*, as if righteousness consisted in negatives. "Why," says the man charged with being a sinner worthy of death, "why, I never hurt anybody in my life; I never committed a sin in my life—that is, you know, a *real* sin. You don't mean that I should be shut out of heaven were I now to die."

Perhaps the man puts great restraint upon himself, and is really at a great deal of trouble not to do wrong. He keeps himself shut in very closely, even more so than many a real Christian does; but if he be not right at the springs of life, he is on the way to eternal ruin just as surely as is the thief or murderer, though on a different charge, and though he is, as far as this world goes, a far better man.

But what ship-owners would justify the captain who should say to them, upon returning from some foreign land, "Here is your ship in the same order as when I took her. I have not harmed her, nor used her for unlawful or piratical purposes. *She is empty, to be sure;* I have done no business for you; but here is that which is yours."

God has sent men out upon the sea of time. They are freighted as no ship ever was. Do you think that he will exonerate them if they dare to go up before him with a plea like that just urged? Our talents must be improved, that at his coming he may receive his own with usury.

It is a man's duty to bring the influence of love to God to bear on every faculty of his soul, that it may be educated and expanded thereby. A man should live in every part of himself, and not be confined to one, two, or six apartments. The world calls a man made or ruined when he has made or lost—what? Wife, children, character, honor, reason? Oh, no—not these; but *money! That's* the thing in which the world makes "the life" of man to consist. Ships are made in various compartments, each air and water-tight, so that when a rock dashes through the bows of the hull, the good ship does not sink, because there are enough other compartments to buoy her up till she gets where she can be overhauled for repairs; but men who have naturally the means of outfloating all the storms, and all the leakages of life, allow most of their compartments to become ruinous for want of use and care. And then, when into the one, or perhaps two or three compartments where they do live, bursts the sunken reef, they are foundered at once. The waters dash in upon them, and they are gone—sunk like a bullet in the sea.

And for this they will be brought into judgment. No man has any right to live in his animal nature, or in his affections, in his tastes and sentiments, in his reason and intellect, or even in his moral nature, to the undue depression of the rest of himself. He should open his whole house, and let light stream into and gleam from the windows of every apartment. Ye who live otherwise are dead while you live. But Christ can give you life. Come unto him.

Make it clear that Christ on earth, with his fathomless love, his unutterable pity, his divine gentleness, and quick and tender notice of all appeals from the humble and poor, was different, in *kind*, from what he *is* in heaven—prove that he acted from design, more than from the impulse of character, and that now the *tenderness* of that strange love and pity is no more, and you take away my Lord, and I know not where ye have laid him. You have robbed me of my God. But now I look upon the story of his acts on earth, when he was, in some sort, fettered by flesh, and the laws which are the masters of flesh, and I say, "If his pity, and his patience, and his love, were such as this while here, what *must they be* now, in their full expansion?"

Christ came to die for our sins; but he came also to show us *what is the character of God*—to teach us, by lessons that we can understand, *what sort of disposition* he has who made us; and now, instead of wishing to go back 1800 years, in order to sit at his feet in Jerusalem, let us rejoice that every year brings us nearer to the hour when we shall go, not to Jesus hampered by fleshly laws, and shrouded as lights are from the eyes of the sick—but to our Saviour glorified and waiting to welcome his children and his brothers to their long-sought home.

I would have loved to listen to my Saviour as he taught upon the plains, or on the mountains, or in the cities of Judea; I would have loved to sit at his feet, to watch his looks as he uttered the blessed words that are recorded; I would have loved to speak with him, face to face—to have seen his smile—to have touched his hands; but, thank God! I can do *better* than that—I can have him, and can hold him in my heart of hearts, as that sweet Friend and Comforter, who could not come down to earth till the *man*, Christ Jesus, was received up into heaven. By love I am conjoined to him, and I feel his soul touch my soul. Thus I can abide with him until I see him, face to face, in heaven.

It seems a hard thing to realize, that so great and high a being, and one so holy as God is, should trouble himself at all about man—a worm—one of these little angling worms that crawls out of his earthy hole, and suns himself a moment, and then crawls in again. But if even the hairs of our heads are all numbered—if he takes notice of *hair*, than which nothing seems more worthless, 'tis a lifeless thing that we cut and throw away—a mere appendage, the *fringe of a man*—what notice must God take of *our living hearts;* our thoughts, which are but the souls of things? We can no longer believe that thoughts and hearts are a matter of small moment to him who made us. He knows us each one by name, by disposition, by character, and he loved us before we were born. Now when he asks us to love and trust in him, he only asks what we know perfectly well *how* to do—what, ever since we were born, we have been doing, only not towards *him*. Didn't we love our mother? Was it *hard* to love her? Don't we trust our friends? Is it hard to trust them?

But where is there mother, or father, or friend, like God? And *do* you say, "It is hard to love and trust in him?" Or do you say: "*I* believe in fore-ordination, and am waiting 'God's time.'"

Fore-ordination! that is a shameful sham. God's time is "now," he never has any other time. Fore-ordination is nothing for you to meddle with, any more in religious than in money-making matters. In each it is in equal force, but 'tis God's business, not yours. If you *will* meddle with it, you deserve to get befogged and puzzled, though there's nothing against, but everything for you in it. But let it alone, if it troubles you.

What farmer, when the sun runs high, and the earth is ready for the seed, and the small rain and the dew are coming on the earth, says: "I believe in fore-ordination; I shall not take the trouble to plant. If I'm to have a harvest, I *shall* have one."

Or what merchant, when he goes to his store in the morning, says: "If I'm to have a good large heap of money in my till to-night, I *shall* have it there. No need for me to trouble myself to please customers, I believe in fore-ordination."

Men are not fools enough for this in temporal concerns, though plenty of them are so in regard to the interests of their immortal souls. No, when they see God working for them *in nature*, they take hold, with a right good will, and work too. And, as a general thing, they gain the blessing for which they strive. In other words, they do, in these minor matters, "work with God," to will and to do of his own good pleasure; but when it comes to spiritual work, they hold quickly back, and exclaim: "Oh! fore-ordination!" But this will be no plea for them, when they come forth from their graves; and when, from mountain and valley, and from the dark waves of the sea, they lift up their blanched faces to their Judge. Of all the myriads who will stand before him, there will not be *one* who will have a word to say—they will "be speechless." For *five dollars* a man will appeal to a higher court. He will go from court to court, sooner than lose "*his rights.*" He will have new trials, if such a thing can be accomplished, and spend three times the sum for which he is contending, sooner than he will submit to be *wronged* out of it. Men do not suffer injustice tamely, but here, where *all* that is of value to the never-dying soul is at stake, here, just upon the edge of the everlasting and most dreadful woe; here, where, if there was *one* single consideration which would tell for them, they would be most patiently and gladly heard, there will not be found one—not one—who shall have the assurance to utter a single syllable.

So clear will be to them the utter folly and willfulness of their self-ruin, that when sentence is pronounced, they will turn in dead silence from the face of Him who sought them all their lives, and veiling their faces, they will take the plunge, from which he *could not* save them. There will be but one expression, and one wail through all that endless falling, and that will be: "Soul, thou hast destroyed thyself."

Becoming a Christian is not becoming better than one's neighbor; it is becoming better than one's self. It has no reference whatever to other people. No one need to feel, when his neighbor becomes a Christian, "That man has set up to be better than we are now, we will therefore watch him, and see how his saintship gets along."

The language of a man standing here to enter the church is not, as many suppose, "I have become so good that I think it will do for me to join myself to Christians." Far from it; his language is, "I have come to see that I am so wicked and so helpless that I cannot stand alone. I am not fit to stand out in the world. I shall certainly perish there. Oh! brethren, I have got my eyes open to my danger and my sin; I have had a vision of the Lord Jesus Christ, of his love and pity for me. I am touched with love for him. I would be fashioned by him; but I dare not stand alone. If you can help me, if there is any safety among you which in the world I do not know, for the love of God receive me, and hold me up until I am able to sustain myself."

There are men who come into this church who are a great deal worse, in many respects, than some others whom I would not vote to admit as members, simply because the first I believe to be Christians, and the latter not.

Suppose five brothers went West to farms, bought here; when they got there, one found his farm to be a swamp; another found his to be full of stumps and rocks, with a poor soil when he got at it; another found his rather better, but still poor enough; a fourth found his good land, but uncleared; while the fifth had a farm on the rolling prairie, with a rich, dark soil that only needed seed to yield abundantly.

At the end of a year, the man who owned the marsh has, by great effort and unremitting industry, got his land drained, manured, and a few acres of it under cultivation; the second has progressed a little further, though with less labor; the third, still further; the fourth has, with one quarter the pains and expense of the first, got four times as much done; while the fields of the fifth are laden with a rich harvest. He is making money the first year. One, judging from appearances of the merits of these farmers, might say the man who owns the fifth farm is the best farmer. I tell you, nay. *He* is the man for work and for courage who has struggled through the disadvantages of that first farm, and has made it *begin* to bear fruit.

There are some men who are born of a good stock; they have well balanced minds, good natural dispositions, and are educated in the very hot-beds of piety. When such are converted there can be but little change in their conduct. The springs and motives of life are touched, and what before was done as unto man, or from a mere sense of duty or propriety, now flows from love to God. Men look at such persons and say, "Well, they *ought* to go into the church; they will be an honor to it." But when the poor, crooked, crabbed, ill-conditioned, ill-constructed sinner, who is so bad that it needs a whole conversion for every faculty in him; who is possessed not only of seven devils, but of seven devils for every one of his powers, comes humbly saying, "The love of Christ has touched even *my* heart—oh help me to grow into his image—receive even me unto his table," men say, "Away with him. He'll be no credit to the church."

Now when such a man really does get his own consent to be a Christian, and sets resolutely about it, he has to *work* for it. He *does* have "a work to do." It takes not one quarter of the religion to make perfect saints of men who by nature have almost everything done for them, that it does to render this other one even decent.

Emphatically, "The first *shall* be last, and the last first."

There are men who dread religion, because they think it circumscribes them.

Doubtless the life of a mere *professor* of religion *is* a life of circumscription ; but to one who has the love of God within him, there is freedom such as no other man can know

What is there of pleasure or of joy, that is worthy of a man, that *I* may not have ?

Is the air less free, the earth less beautiful to me, because I am a child of God, and can rejoice in my sonship to him who created all things ?

Is *love* less to me, because I know and feel that it is to last forever ?

Are social pleasures less keenly relished, or friendship less valued by me, because I know that they will be eternal, and are to brighten forever beneath the smile of my God ?

I tell you there is no man that has half the right to the things *that now are*, that *he* has who by faith and love has laid hold upon the things which are to come. To a Christian, earth is both substance and shadow. It is, in its better joys, a hint of the perfect joys to come. It is a glass into which one may look and see reflections of eternity. It is an utter impossibility to have any true and continuous satisfaction in life, unless you do feel that you have the love of the Giver of Life; unless you love him. If that consciousness is yours, though you be shorn of all other joys, *that* will sustain you; but the probability is, that all other joys will grow firm, founded upon that one; for ours are not the days when religion arrayed all earthly power against men!

THERE are men who will not seek for religion when no one else is seeking, because they don't want to be thought singular—shame working through the organ of approbativeness—and then, when a revival comes, they won't seek it, because they don't want to get excited, and go with a crowd—shame working through self-esteem—and thus, between those two guards, warding them off from the door of salvation, the poor fools perish.

MANY a man, awakening to a sense of his wickedness and trying to do better, finds himself so much worse that he cries out in terror of himself.

If any of you who are unconverted doubt of your need of the help of Christ to curb your sins, just try for a few days to do it alone. They will give you work of it! You'll say you never were so bad before. You never *were* so universally in rebellion. While your will goes with your selfish or evil desires there is no conflict—or none that makes much stir and dust. I don't know as water would ever make any noise if it were allowed to flow unobstructed; but put rocks in its way, let logs stick up in the current, dam it up, or in any way obstruct it, and then see—such a noise, such a commotion, such a determined overflowing as it makes; and it *will* get out somewhere. So with yourselves—as long as your heart is let to flow undisturbedly hellward, there may be but little trouble; you may hardly be conscious that you are a rebel at all; but lay on the bands, mark out the bounds, hold in the lines—and what then? Why, then you will see how desperate is your case, and will soon discover that there is none but the Son of God that can help you. Then do not be afraid to go to him, because you fear you can't hold out; take the first step and he'll help you; when you fail and fall he'll always forgive you; if you are strong, and *never give over* trying to work *with* him *against* your besetting sins, he has promised, "I will never leave thee nor forsake thee."

Oh! friends bound with me to the judgment, put not this matter aside. I feel that I could plead with you till the sun goes down, my heart is so in it. Talk not, I beseech you, as you go from here, of the speaker, the gestures, or the striking passages—talk of the passages that *struck*, or go thinking silently of what is to come to every one of you. Let the sun go down, and when it is set we will pursue the subject, and may God direct his own word and truth to the salvation of souls.

If there is joy in heaven over *one* sinner that repents, I don't know what the angels will do now that men everywhere are taking the kingdom of heaven by force.*

How marvellous is that part of the nature of God that permits him, while himself so pure and holy, to take tenderly to his bosom, and comfort with his love, creatures so full of sin as we are. Sinners unregenerated are perplexed by the joy and courage of Christians who cannot but be conscious that they are yet very imperfect, sinful beings. They do not see how we dare to trust in Christ while we yet do wrong. If we did no wrong we should have no further need of Christ. Believing on him is not instantaneous cure from sin; it is release from the curse and bondage of it, and surety that the cure is coming. Christians are like men with some disease upon them; who have faith in the physician that has engaged to heal them, and they lend themselves with earnestness to the work of getting well. Re-

* March, 1858.

lapses grieve them, but do not discourage. They rise up as often as they fall down. They groan and long to be delivered from the burden of death which is upon them, and they know that deliverance will come.

Sinners, until awakened, don't know that they are burdened. They are like sick men with no shelter, no physician, no nurse, growing worse and worse forever. When they *are* awakened, their first thought and effort is to try to get *worthy* to come to Christ. Could they do that, which none ever can do, they would not *need* him. The point at which a man comes to see that he is utterly evil and helpless, and consequently turns to Christ as his *only* hope and help, *is the point at which conversion takes place.* On one side of this point a man is a sinner without hope; on the other side *he is a Christian.* A sinner still, to be sure; but with a certainty of healing, rescue, and salvation.

MEN take the world, filled, *stuffed* as it is with all good and beautiful things, very much as gipsies would take some glorious mansion, furnished with rare taste, and adorned with masterpieces of art. The chief room they would attempt to occupy would be the kitchen, and they would take the treasures of manuscripts, in which were written wonderful secrets of invention and science, and the solutions of great mysteries, to kindle the fire under their dinner pot. They would like the pictures, because they had oil in them and would burn the faster. Thus blind to the higher uses of the things of the world are men. And it is the way of God never to stir one step from his path to show them better. He has given them the faculty to find out, and there he leaves them. In the physical economy of the world there is provision for all physical wants; but they lie for the most part hidden. Not till the earth is scarified and rent, forced open and bored into, does she disclose or yield her treasures. Near acres of wheat, men may starve; by the side of forests and beds of fuel, they may freeze. God will not move one inch, or one finger to save man, if he will not, with what he has already done for him, save himself. So in the spiritual world, provision for all men is plenteously made; but they will be allowed to perish unless they come and appropriate it.

All things are to be had for the taking; nothing without.

Let no man *dare* to think, "God, the gentle and merciful, will save me, whether I come to his terms or not." The whole analogy of life is against the thought. God will not save you, body or soul, except in appointed ways. It is turn or die.

Unutterably dreadful is the thought of eternal death. Eternal! It is absolutely suffocating. I have felt my whole nature revolt against the horror of the conception; and I *would have* disbelieved it if I could. But no! it is true—it is an awful truth, and the mentions of it in the Bible are not so much threats as merciful disclosures of what lies at the end of the sinner's course, that he may be induced to flee for refuge to the hope set before him. Even if the passages regarding hell could be made to mean something else it would not unsettle my faith in this doctrine. It would never be enough for me to take these passages of the eternal word, and, placing them in the rack, wrench and torture them until I made the poor words shriek forth some other meaning, unless I could see that the Lord, who is dominant over the natural as well as the spiritual world, turned aside in that for the sake of helping those who in *natural* things will not "come" to what he has appointed for help and healing.

The ages have rolled and rolled, and through them all the sound of the earth's groaning has gone up to God, and he has never stirred. Man *must* avail himself of what has been done for him, *or he must die.* God has done *all* that he will ever do in the matter of providing means for salvation. The rest is left to man.

No man has any business to try to be a Christian secretly. The light of love is not one for him to hide under a bushel. And, usually, a man's first duty after conversion, is to make the fact known to the very persons from whom he most wishes to keep it.

I think no sufficient reason has ever yet been given for the great reserve felt by us toward those persons who are most dear to us. We shrink more from saying to our parents, wives, husbands and children, the things that lie deepest, than to any one else in the world. Why this should be so it is not easy to understand.

I can very well understand how and why a man hates to say to his business partner, with whom he has long been engaged in cheating people—"I have become a Christian." I know that it *must* make him twinge, and feel *particularly* uncomfortable to stand up and own this, and to have his partner say, "Ah! well, how is it to be now about those profits that we have hitherto shared between us? Those *extra* profits—profits that we got *in those ways, you know.* Am I to have them all now?"

I can imagine how a liquor-dealer would feel to own his conversion, and to hear, "Well, what are you going to do?—going to join the church?"

"Yes, if they'll have me."

"Going to set up family prayer?"

"Yes, I shall pray in my family."

"Well, what *else* are you going to do?"

"Why, I shall try to do my duty."

"Yes, *but about the liquor*, I mean."

No doubt all this comes hard. But these things have got to be met and dealt with. If a man is noble he will say, "Not only will I put out my eye if it offends me, but I will put out both eyes; for I have got two eyes opened in my soul that are worth more to see with than forty * bodily eyes."

Sins against society—which is money—are felt to be very sinful, by those who have the money and who mean to keep it. Strike the side of a bee-hive and see how the bees will swarm out, and buzz and buzz to defend themselves. Go on to Wall street or Broadway with any indulgences for financial sins, and there will be equal buzzing there. *Crimes* are owned to be sins indeed, because they touch the *material* interests of men, or hurt their affections—their selfishness; but when you pronounce men sinful in the higher, spiritual sense, they cannot feel anything about it. There are greater sins

* "Forty" and "five hundred" are Mr. Beecher's favorite, and most frequently mentioned numbers. He seems to have exempted them from his general dislike to figures.

and smaller sins, it is true; but *all* that is not of faith and love is sin. Jonathan as truly broke the law of his father the king, by tasting the honey on the end of his rod, as if he had slaughtered an ox and partaken of its flesh. As long as a man commits no *crime* he don't feel himself condemned, though his spiritual nature be dumb, dead, petrified.

There are seasons peculiarly fitted for becoming a Christian. There are no feelings or sentiments of which the soul is capable but what have their tides. They ebb and flow like the sea. This seems to be one of the laws of our nature.

There are times when the popular tide sets towards religion; when all outward circumstances, as well as all inward yearnings, conspire to invite and even press the sinner towards God.

Some persons object to revivals, saying, "We don't believe in feeling and impulse. We think religion too serious a matter to be entered upon hastily. We think it requires calm consideration."

Well, you man, twenty, thirty, forty years old, you with the grey hairs fast covering you, *how much longer* do you wish to consider? Remember that Death sometimes strikes without much consideration. What if he strikes you? Where will your calm thoughts be then?

Truly, 'tis a wise piece of business for a man, hanging by no more than a single hair over the bottomless pit, to say to the friend who throws him a stout rope, "Wait, I must consider calmly of this —I don't believe in being in a hurry." There are some cases where consideration is crime—where deliberation is death. Unutterable fools! that think, and think, and *only* think, upon the borders of perdition. The sands beneath their feet are crumbling and shifting away; but they must think, they say, when one calls to them to run. And so they pause, and perish.

Feelings *ought* to be regarded; sympathetic emotion is good for hearts. As much so in *religion* as elsewhere.

Resist not the spirit when your heart is tender and your thoughts turn in you, and lift themselves up towards God.

WHAT shall we do to be saved? this is now the daily utterance of men's voices. Believe on Christ—drop instantly and forever all known sins—all meannesses, all dishonesties, all unkindnesses, at home and everywhere, all wrong thoughts and evil imaginations. You never can go in at "the strait gate," with any of these clinging to your will.

Do you cry out, "I cannot do this; the work is

too hard for me—if I quit my sins they won't quit me. I cannot say to passion, avarice, selfishness, and pride, 'lie down and move no more;' I *cannot* think right, and act right. I *am not able* to enter the gate if *this* is the way." If you think thus, how comes it that you have been putting off this matter of repentance to a sick-bed, or to old age? If you cannot reform your thoughts and disposition *now*, how can you then? You say truly, you *cannot* reform them, and for this cause you need a Saviour. But you *can* remove them, and turn from them, and consecrate your whole body and soul to him, and *he* will reform you by aiding all your efforts. He will forgive as often as you break down, if you carry a steadfast purpose to conquer *self*, for the sake of his love. He will not fail you, if you are sincere in seeking him; but he will abhor your offering if you do not mean to make clean work with yourself by laying open your whole heart and life to his influence.

Many shall seek to enter in, and shall not be able; but *not because of any trouble in the gate*, or in the Lord that stands at the head of the way, but because they try to carry in their barrels of spirit, or their selfishness, or their vile and evil dispositions and habits. Such can never enter. No rich man can go through that gate carrying with him his usury, or his exorbitant rents, wrung from sweating and groaning tenants. No unjust judge can go through with his oppressions. But there never was, and never will be, a naked, trembling soul, sincerely sorry for sin, and heartily desirous of escaping from its power, and to be made white in the blood of sprinkling, for which there is not *abundant* room. And yet " Many *shall* seek to enter in and shall not be able." Many are the secret sins of heart and life whose clinging shall prevent the sinner.

Ships, when the tide rises and sets strongly in any direction, sometimes turn and seem as if they would go out upon it. But they only head that way, and move from side to side, swaying and swinging without moving on at all. There *seems* to be nothing to hinder them from sailing and floating out to sea ; but there *is* something.

Down under the water a great anchor lies buried in the mud. The ship cannot escape. The *anchor* holds her. And thus are men holden, by the cords of their own sins. They go about trying to discover some way to be forgiven, and yet keep good friends with the devils that are in them. And this they call "being serious." It is almost all self-will fighting against the Spirit of God. Now, let men be honest with themselves, and if they think their sins, any or all of them, are better than the love of God and the salvation of their souls, why stick to them, that is all; and give up thinking; but if they feel that the redemption of the soul *is* precious, and that it ceaseth *forever*, let them abandon all that hinders it, and begin at once to work with God for their own salvation. What they *can* do they *must* do, or be lost, and that is, stop all wrong doing that they can stop; what they *can't*, Christ will attend to, reforming their interior dispositions by the love which he will shed abroad in their souls. Turn ye, turn ye, for why *will* ye die? Now is the accepted time—all things now are ready. The Lord has brought you nigh unto him, and on every side of you men are hastening to make their peace with God. Beware how you let this opportunity pass. You may not have another. What would you say when some great steamer had run aground where there was but one tide in a year that would float her, if, upon the day before that tide came, her officers got together for a council, and decided that as there was but one tide a year, and they didn't believe in taking advantage of extraordinary times, that they should make no effort to get the ship off. When the tide rose, surging and booming about the ship, if they had got up steam and set all sail, and worked her giant wheels, grating, groaning, and reluctant, she might have moved and struggled off into deep soundings. But they let the flood tide pass; and the water sank away from the ship's keel, and she cracked and parted asunder.

Anon the beautiful and mighty ship was floating, but it was plank by plank, and spar by spar.

What, I ask, would you think of those officers?

But what is a ship when compared to a human soul; which, being created, is to go step by step with God throughout eternity; forever rising in purity and love, or forever sinking into the blackness of darkness?

When you and I, my hearers, stand in the fore front of the judgment ranks to hear our doom, when all above us and around is the glory and the brightness of the Holy City, and all beneath us is the blackness of despair, you will not accuse me of exaggeration in saying to you that there are none so unwise, so blind, so miserably foolish and desperate, as those who, for *any* cause, do not *first* attend to the safety of their own souls. With all my power I warn you; with all my strength I entreat you; with all my skill I will aid you. Oh! seek ye the Lord while he may be found.

I OFTEN find, in talking with people, that they are in a state amounting to, or which ought to amount to, conversion. They see and feel their sinfulness and need of Christ; they are prepared to cut off limbs or pluck out eyes in his service. They tell me with tears, that they have moments of great affectional yearning towards him; and yet they don't "go off." They are waiting to get something more, although they don't exactly know what, aboard. When I go and talk with them they seem all right; but I leave them, and they stand still. I find them in the same spot day after day. Now, there's no use in my going to talk with such people. They must get themselves to work; they must begin to *do* something, as well as *feel* so much. Let them enter upon the Christian life at once; perform every known duty—stop every known sin.

Here is a clock; the works are all right, the hands point to the right time, and 'tis all properly wound up. Everything is in prime order, and ready to go. But it *don't* go. What is the matter? You look at it an hour hence, and the hands have not stirred. You move them forward and leave it, and the next hour you have got to set them again. This sort of work you may keep at forever. As long as the pendulum is not moved the clock won't go. Let *that* begin to tick, and all is at once right and busy. Now, let those persons who are all wound up just begin to tick. Start your pendulum and the trouble is over.

THERE are many persons, and I find them chiefly women, who do not experience any deep throes or trouble in entering the right way.

Their conviction of sin is not such as catches them and plunges them headlong into agonies and horrors of great darkness; but they look on Christ and love him, and at once accept him. They have a *real*, but not particularly powerful knowledge that they are lost without him. They are conscious that they are poor and sinful, very much as a little child is conscious that he is ignorant, and they go to Jesus for riches and righteousness very much as the child goes to school for learning. The child has faint ideas of how utter is his ignorance; but after he begins to learn he sees it more and more. These penitents are but faintly aware how deep is their sinfulness until they have begun to see as God sees, which is not for some time after he has blessed them with his adoption. Often the fact that there was so little struggle in their conversion has caused them to doubt its genuineness; and so they have got into great darkness; but they must remember that God leads men to him in ways best suited to their own natures and dispositions, and while they who are naturally passionate and willful, who have more strength than tenderness in their dispositions, are often seized and rent like him out of whom went the furious devil, and are left wallowing upon the earth before they will look to their Saviour, those who are of a gentle and loving disposition, whose will has been trained to submission, and who have lived chiefly in their higher nature all their days, will not, they *ought* not to, find it hard to come to Jesus Christ to put their arms about his neck, and tell him with gushing love, that they give themselves, body and soul, into his keeping.

Blessed are they who can look upon the Saviour, and so instantly feel his goodness and beauty, and be so penetrated by his wonderful love, that with hardly a thought of self, they run to him and offer him themselves. This is the highest form of conversion. Conviction will be sure to be felt by such hearts as these every time the thought of what it is to grieve such a Saviour touches them. And the longer they live the worse will their own sins, and all sins, look to them. Let no one then, who has enough conviction to honestly desire to forsake sin, and to understand that in Christ lies *all* his help, wait for more or for a deeper feeling. If the wind is blowing two knots an hour, don't wait till it blows ten knots before you start your ship. If there's enough wind to start on, *start*—be off. If you want to come to Christ, *come*, don't wait *for anything.* If you can't feel as bad as you want to, don't stop on that account. When you've learned to love God, you'll feel more than you can ever imagine now.

When serious persons ask me what to read, I am accustomed to say: "There is a little old book called Matthew's Gospel, which I think would suit your case. And there are three others which are just as good: Mark, Luke, and John."

Don't go to the side helps of commentaries until after conversion. I think that commentaries for inquirers are like the spider webs of fifty years over windows, for sight. You must brush them all away before you can see clearly. No book in the wide world has been so be-webbed as the Bible. Commentaries are very well for those who need helps in dates, or in sacred history; but let the awakened sinner go straight to the fountain-head of truth—the Bible. And is the reading all? Oh! no, read *praying*. And here again is where there are many and deplorable mistakes made. The inquirer, and the young convert, try to pray too long and not often enough. They try praying as they have always heard the deacon and the minister pray, or as their father does; and then they get into great distress because their "thoughts wander." That is *the best thing about* it. When they attempt to do what for them is as impossible as for a lisping babe to converse like a philosopher, their thoughts *will* and ought to wander. If this were otherwise, they would but the better play the hypocrite before God by praying things for which they don't and can't feel the need, and in cold set forms of chilling reverence. Now we have a model for the prayers of beginners, and 'tis this: "God be merciful to me a sinner." You *can* feel all of that; you see it begins abruptly; and it ends when the man is done.

No "Oh! thou mighty, mysterious and everlasting Lord." No "Forever and ever, amen!" about *that.*

Let it be a lesson to you, beginner. Pray what you feel, and *not one word more.*

Read on; and if you are perplexed, and your thoughts look up, say: "Lord, I can't understand this. I pray thee help me." Then stop, *if you are done.*

Read on; and if a scene, or an action, or saying, of your Saviour touches the fount of feeling, let that feeling out, saying freely: "Dear Lord, I love thee, for thou truly *art* worthy!"

And so on through his whole recorded life, and through your own life. Be instant in prayer. Warm, true, impulsive, and affectionate in communion with your God.

The utterances of real feeling only are acceptable to him. Forced prayer, or insincerity in prayer, is like foul odor in his nostrils.

It is enough that he is willing to forgive us our sins, and to excuse the imperfections of our earnest prayers; let us spare him *mockery* added to sin.

If we can't feel like praying for everybody, and for everything, or like praying when we think we ought to pray, and if we are sorry that we feel so dull and prayerless, let us say *that* to God, and keep silence till we can feel more. God's heart is like our hearts—like a parent's heart. Our hearts are made by the pattern of his.

How would a man like to have his own children observe only set times of coming to converse with him? Coming *from a sense of duty* at that? How would he like to have them arrange all that they have to say in set and studied forms, very respect ful, perhaps, very laudatory, very humble and devout, but *very* heartless?

Think you that what would cut you to the heart, coming from your own offspring, does not at all hurt him whose tenderness is the ocean out of which your *drop* is drawn?

When I was in Paris, I used to rise early and sit at my open window. I always knew when the stores beneath me were open, for one was a flower store, and from its numberless roses, and heaps of mignonnette, arose such sweet, *sweet* fragrance, that it proclaimed what was done. It seems to me that Christians should be as a flower store, and that the odor of sanctity should betray them wherever they are. Not that they should go about obtruding themselves and their actions on others, with the *cant* of usefulness, but that they should live the purity and joy of religion, so that men might see the desirableness of it, both for the sake of nobleness, and for the enjoyment both of this world and that which is to come.

CONVICTION comes upon men in a thousand different ways; sometimes a little child climbs upon his father's knee, and says, looking up earnestly, "Pa, why don't you pray?" I tell you, there's many a man would rather a pistol were snapped in his face, than to hear that question from a little child.

Do you say: "I want to be a Christian, but I'm waiting to be convicted of sin; it isn't right for me to do anything till I've felt myself to be a sinner"—then to you I am sent to say, you have no right to wait for *anything*. Begin, this instant, to love God, and to act like a Christian.

"But I *can't*," you say.

Ah! have you come to that knowledge already? That is conviction of helplessness in the direction of goodness. Just go earnestly and perseveringly to work to act right and to think right, and you'll get conviction enough.

You may stand still and wait for it, looking into your own heart to see what you are, *forever*, and not get it; but just try living right, by the rules Christ gives, and it will come upon you, so that you shall cry out, "God be merciful, and *help* me; for there is no good thing in me."

It's everybody's duty to begin *at once* to live like a Christian; and when they find how they fail of all they want to do, they will be convicted; and when they give themselves utterly into the hands of Christ, they will be converted; that *is* conversion, it won't be *becoming perfect*, but it is the *first step* towards perfection. You must always keep trying to be good, just as hard as if you had all to do for yourself; but you must no more be discouraged by failures than if you had nothing to do, for you have *always*, night and day, an advocate with the Father—one who is righteous, though you are not—and who will *never* leave nor forsake those who trust in him. Therefore, come boldly to him, asking for grace to help in all times of need, and *knowing*, that though you fall, you shall rise again.

SOME people seem to make a merit of great anxiety for their friends ; now there is no merit, and no use, and there is positive harm in more anxiety for them than will excite you to do all that you can to influence them aright. When that is done, and you have committed them to God, then go away, and *feel happy* about them.

We are a singing church, and when we are dead, and men come and scrape the moss from our graves, they will say: "These were Christians who sang much."

You are planting seeds for the future as you sing these hymns. Were you to go away to Oregon next year, this book, out of which we have all sung together, would be a hundred books to you; how it would make you remember these morning meetings, these lectures, these Sabbaths.

While Brother —— was praying,* the words, "Come up hither," came to me. As I wondered what it meant, instantly it opened up to me in this way.

Suppose that I had gone away from here for years, and came back to find my daughter living in some low, obscure place, bound out to hard labor

* In a prayer-meeting.

for people who took no notice of her; or worse, noticed her only to abuse her. Suppose my son were in another place, half clothed, half fed, and suffering all manner of ill treatment. And thus with all my children.

What should I be likely to do? Should I not at once set about lifting them out of such situations, and getting them up where I was, I should say to them,

"Come up, my children; you were not born to live down there. Your place is where I am. Come up here to me; here is where you belong."

Well, this is what God is doing to men. He has a few, a very few children living in the high places of spiritual life—those regions of hope and love where he himself dwells.

But most of his earthly family dwell far below, and he is constantly coming down to seek for them.

He looks in the region of awe and reverence, in the region of conscience, in that of despondency and fear; yes, he even goes down cellar after them, and sometimes can't find them even there. But wherever he does find them, he says to them:

"Come up hither—come up into the region of warmth and love, where your Father dwells. You were not made to live down there. This is where you belong. Come up hither."

We must not settle down indolently to wait for God to make fruit grow in us. He never does anything for us in regard to character without our coöperation. Work out your own salvation with fear and trembling, not servile fear, or abject trembling, but with such eagerness as men often feel in an engrossing work they are so eager about that their nerves quiver a little. It is in doing our duties, and bearing our trials and vexations, that Christ is with us, and will dwell in us for our comfort; but he will not dwell in us in any such way as that we shall have no more trouble and pain in struggling with our passions, our failings, our avarice, our pride, and all our besetting sins. It is by fighting and overcoming these that we get to be fruitful. "Work out your own salvation with fear and trembling, for it is God that worketh in you, both to will and to do of his own good pleasure." These things God put together, and no man ought to put them asunder. As you climb difficult hills your prospects will be brighter and clearer; but not until you have gained the highest peak of experience will you be able to see, from horizon to horizon, the presence with you of God; and then you will soon begin to descend; for it is generally not until near death that the Christian gets a view like this.

The great truth which God is driving through our times, as with a chariot of fire, is *the importance of man!* When this truth comes up to the church, does she welcome it? No! oh *no*—she cannot attend to new comers; she is busy in the smoke-house of theology, dusting the flitches of old truth which have hung there for ages.

A grand mistake of the old reasoners in their arguing for the goodness of God, was that they tried to prove that in the world there is more evidence of design for happiness than there is of design for pain.

Now that position cannot be maintained. There is just as much evidence of a design to produce pain as to produce pleasure.

For every adaptation for pleasure that you will show me I will undertake to show you one for pain. This life is clearly rudimentary. Men are here to be hammered into something of worth in the next state of existence. Pleasure is to be desired or expected but as incidental. Earth is not the place for *pleasure.* It is the place where men are fashioned for eternity. A piano factory is not the place to go to in order to hear music. Suppose a man were to start for some great piano manufactory, with the expectation of being enchanted when there by innumerable Thalbergs.

He goes along dreaming of the divine harmonies which will greet him when he approaches the place where these sweet-toned instruments are made.

He anticipates as much more of delight than Thalberg had given him, as there are more instruments in the factory than were on the boards of the concert hall.

"I am going to the place where all those pianos are made," he says, as he hastens on. "They turn out hundreds of them in a day. Oh! how will all sweet, bewildering sounds entrance my senses when I draw near. Hymns and songs of never-wearying melody will leap out at me from every door and window."

He comes in sight of the building, and instead of hymns and choral melodies, he hears harsh noises. There are heavy poundings, gratings, sawings, and raspings. There are legs, uncouth and clumsy, to be worked into proper size and gracefulness. There are strings to be tried, and separate parts to be fitted and knocked together; there are great, heavy packing-boxes to be made, and various other awkward and noisy work to be done.

Tools are thumping about; cords and tackling rattling; plenty of confounding noises, but *no music.*

The man stands and sees the workmen ply the

hammer, and saw, and file, and punch, and chisel, and auger; he sees dust, boards, and shavings flying in all directions. Clatter and clatter surround him.

From the windows come broken bits of board, wire, and iron; also all the different notes of racket and din; but he hears no sweet melody.

Then the man says in astonishment, "Do they call *this* a piano manufactory—this confused place, full of all jangling noises? No, no; this is no piano producing establishment. This is only a dusty and noisy workshop."

Yes, it *is* a workshop, where are being fashioned the instruments, which, when touched by skillful fingers, have power to enchant the world.

But it is not the platform on which they are to be played. Not *there* are they to give forth their sweet harmonies.

We are in the workshop of humanity. We see evidences of this, turn which way we will.

Evidences are numerous of a design of *pounding* us. We must feel the mallet and the saw; the punch and the bore. We must be split, and ground, and worked smooth. The pumice and the sand-paper are for us, also, as well as for the things we fashion; and *at last*, when we are all set together, polished, and attuned, we shall be played upon by the music-waking influences of heaven.

Fighting faults is the most discouraging thing in the world.

When corn reaches a certain height, no more weeds can grow among it. The corn overshadows and grows them down. Let men fill themselves full of good things. Let them make their love and purity and kindness to grow up like corn, that every evil and noxious thing within them may be overshadowed and die.

Men are not put into this world to be everlastingly fiddled on by the fingers of joy.

Those persons who do most good are least conscious of it. The man who has but a single virtue or charity is very much like the hen that has but one chicken. *That solitary chicken* calls forth an amount of clucking and scratching that a whole brood seldom causes.

Sometimes, when mists conceal the bed of a river in which work is to be done, or which is to be forded, men are placed in the tops of trees along its banks, that they may look across, and sing out to those below, "Go on; you are in the right way. We see the other shore, though you cannot. March on." Thus has God put look-outs in the trees along the banks of the River of Death.

Not many—many are not needed; but in every Christian community there are some men who can see clear across the misty waters to the shores of heaven. God says to them, "Bear witness. Call cheerily out unto your brothers who cannot see for the fog through which they are walking. Tell them that all is right. Tell them not to flag or fear; that they are in the right way, and that the shore is not hard to gain if, only, they *press on*."

One such man in the tree will do for the encouragement of hundreds below in the river.

There was but one Moses to the thousand of Israelites that entered the Jordan.

YOUNG Christian, do you want a prophecy of the future? I'll tell you how to get it. In the first place, let the future *alone*, then call to your heart, "Heart, art ready for each large or small duty of to-day? If your heart answers, as bells do him who strikes them, if it cry lustily, and with no tarrying, "Ready, aye, ready!" and if this is, day by day, its sincere cry, you have your prophecy. You will not be troubled about dying when you *are* dying.

When Joseph sent for his father to come to Egypt, he sent men, and chariots, and horsemen, and provisions, all in profuse abundance. He didn't suppose that the old patriarch could journey with only his staff for company, finding himself by the way; and do you think that when God sends for you he will provide *less* bounteously for the journey to his home? No, no; when your work is ended, when your royal day has come, you shall have cause to cry out, in rapturous praise, Sufficient! sufficient! sufficient! is the escort which thou hast provided to bear me over to the Heavenly Land.

No man can go down the path of memory or experience into his own heart, and with the light of God's word look into all its dark chambers, and hidden cavities, and slimy recesses, and not come up with a shudder and a chill, and an earnest cry to God for mercy.

Where Christianity is fruitful of speculations and barren of good conduct, infidels always abound.

It is not death but life that we long for when we sigh to flee away and be at rest.

When we think of the grave, of the chill and ghastliness of death, we cannot say that we are so willing to try it; but when we *leap the grave*, sink the very memory of it, and land safe over in heaven, then, indeed, are we ready, aye, longing to depart.

How skillfully does Paul sail past the two unpleasing points, without touching too hard on either. "It is not that we would be unclothed, but that we would be clothed upon."

It is *not* desirable to be borne away alone, to lie and moulder in the cold, damp grave; but it *is* desirable, soon as may be, to enter heaven.

When you can make an oak out of a mushroom, then, and not till then, you may hope to make a living tree out of that poisonous toadstool, the theatre.

It was, even among the heathen nations, considered a disgrace to be connected with one; and down through all the thousands of years which it has lived since then, it has come with perpetual dishonor on its head.

Men say we *must* be honest; it is our *duty*. But they think there is no duty about being happy any more than about having fine weather. The weather is just as it happens, and so they suppose it is about happiness. But I tell you there is no more positive *command* in the Bible than this reiterated one,

"*Rejoice* in the Lord alway; and *again* I say *rejoice*." And this rejoicing is not to be in pleasure and profit, in good prospects, or in sunny days, but "in the Lord," a joy that shall be independent of circumstances—a joy that men shall be obliged to confess must come of religion. A Christian is indeed allowed to rejoice where other men can; but he is bound to rejoice where other men *cannot*.

Who cannot rejoice when he holds his first-born to his breast? But, Christian, *you* are to rejoice when you bend, with falling tears, over his coffin. Weep! it is your right; but "rejoice in God."

Who cannot rejoice when he walks with his bride smiling beside him? But *you* are to rejoice when she lies stiffened in death on her bier.

Do you say it is impossible for you thus, at will, to banish sorrow, and recall joy?

It is *not* impossible. You cannot do it as you can will your eye to open or shut; but you can do it by controlling the causes of things.

You can live in such abiding consciousness of eternity, that time and the things thereof shall be to you but as pictures hung up in a hall, which may all be taken away without touching you.

When losses come upon you, you may and ought to sorrow for pain of present bereavement, but you should rejoice with a joy which no man may take from you, in the promise that all of yours which is worth having will be restored to you, where it will be dearer and better than ever.

Live so that your peace and joy shall be the "light" that shall shine on men, showing them the power of religion *thus*, rather than by seriousness and gloom of face and temper.

You are not to follow after happiness as an end of life. So sure as you do this, you will *never* be happy. But be happy while you work with God. Ye are the temples of God. Be cheerful while you help your Master Builder to perfect his temple.

Under all discouragements, bear up cheerfully, remembering that it is by trouble that God puts temper into the steel. If it will not bear tempering, it is not worth much. He has promised, once for all, "I will *never* leave thee, nor forsake thee;" and has declared, "There hath not entered into thy heart the joys that are laid up for them that love me." What need we more?

What feeble and ungrateful wretches we are, not to be able to rejoice always, when we have such joys before us.

Much harm has been done by the idea that a certain gloom, and a restriction of the lively emotions, bear some relations to piety.

These bear the same relation to it that rust does to the sword-blade—*they eat into it.*

The command, "Be sober," does not mean be unmirthful.

I WOULD rather break stone on the road, were it not for the disgrace of working in a chain-gang, than to be one of those beings who are so rich that they have nothing to do but to "seek happiness," as they call it.

The "upper class," as they style themselves, are the *flies of humanity*; and if there could be some great fan invented to sweep them all out of the way, it would be a benefit to the world.

The working of such a fan would be a very good business for somebody.

And yet these beings presume to make society's laws. I must repeat, as the only true description of them that I know in the English language Pope's lines—"If the gods be monkeys, what must the people be?"

WHAT does Paul mean in saying, "I am persecuted, but not forsaken?" It's a very pleasant thing, *sometimes*, to be persecuted—it's delicious! When a man has his own house, and his family around him, as much salary as he can spend, and more friends than he knows what to do with, it is a pleasant excitement, when breakfast is over, to open the papers and look to see how he is "persecuted;" but this was not the way with Paul. He was driven out, and hunted up and down; he had neither father, mother, wife, sister, brother, nor constant companion, save his dark-browed jailer—yet he did not feel forsaken. He was troubled on every side, yet not distressed.

As a mailed warrior might stand amid flying darts from Indian bows, feeling them hurtling and rattling against helmet and corselet, and shield, and falling about him like hail, until they were piled a thousand high, and yet smile, saying: "They hit me indeed; I am pelted and shot at of the archers, but I am not *hurt*." So stood Paul in his armor of proof.

A man in the lists fights first with lance and spear; then, dropping these, he seeks in the closer contest, with the shorter dagger, to stab and kill. Then flinging this away closes in the deadlier grapple. Then the two sway and bend, and topple to their fall, each struggling to overthrow his enemy, knowing well that who goes *down* is *the dead man*.

They reel, they stumble, they fall, and at the overthrow one feels the knee of the conqueror on his breast, and sees the deadly steel shortened above his heart. Thus was it with Paul—yet there, lying prostrate in the dust, dying by cruel hands, he uttered his voice, and its triumphant joy comes ringing down the path of ages, to teach *us* how, in the loss of all things, to rejoice in God.

Ah! look not in the throne for strength.

The prisoner in the dungeon was mightier than the king. He that was under the throne was stronger than he that sat upon it.

We are not to seek pain; but when it is sent to us we are not to fret and grumble at it, but try and go cheerfully along, as though we did not feel it. It is for our good, our purification—for nothing is so purifying as pain, if it be rightly borne.

Suppose I could have these faces gathered and brought to me, and could hold them thus, and should ask: "Whose image and superscription is stamped on this face?"

"Care marked this face," would be the (frequent) answer.

"Who marked this one?"

"Fretfulness."

"And this?"

"Selfishness."

"This?"

"Suffering stamped this."

"What this?"

"Lust! lust!"

"And this?"

"Self-will."

"And who stamped this face?" I should ask of one—a rare and sweet one.

"This! why where did you get it? Whose face is this?—how beautiful! It is marked by the sweet peace of a contented spirit." I never saw more than a dozen of these in my life.

THERE are multitudes of men who are like summer vines. They lie along the ground, and reach out a thousand little hands to grasp the stronger shrubs, and if they cannot reach them, they lie upon the ground forever hoof-trodden, dishevelled, and beaten of every storm.

I HAVE heard people say, "What a fortunate circumstance it was that that trouble came to-day, just as I was so well prepared to meet it. I really don't think I could have borne it if it had come at some other time." Very true; you could not. God knew that, and he did not send it upon you until he had prepared you to bear it. It *was* fortunate for you that he thus cared for you; yet you speak as if its coming just at that time were all accidental.

H-h-h-h-m! what a fortunate thing it was for the tree that there *happened* to be a blossom just where the fruit wanted to grow; and what a fortunate thing it was that a bud *happened* to grow just where the blossom wanted to open.

It is a fortunate thing for my head that I've got a neck; and it is a very fine thing for my neck that I've got shoulders, and trunk and limbs under it; and a fine thing for all these that I've got feet to move them all about upon. I don't know what I should have done if things had not *happened* to come just as they did.

These things do not come one whit more along the line of sequences than did your strength made equal to your day.

That was God's promise fulfilled and you refused to see it. Your privilege is to be troubled about *nothing*. "Work well *to-day;* there all your duty lies."

Don't imagine trouble; don't borrow it; don't *die* before your time. When God wants you to die he will show you how to do it easy.

You come to church to be *told how* to be the saint; you go out into the world to *be* it.

There is a question in the air that no set of men, be they of what sect they may, can steer quite clear of in their talk.

This question is sizzling everywhere. Hush it up, cover it down, as you please, it *will* keep bursting out. 'Tis bubbling up on all sides of you. You *must* agitate it.

God is in this thing, doing what I have all along prayed that he would do, viz., working in a way that will make all parties feel that the thing is not of man.

He has overturned the plans both of agitators and of quietists; but still he is putting on the spurs. He is forcing men to agitate the matter; and until they do it, he will agitate *them*.

Order and quiet are good things, when they can be had without the sacrifice of things that are better. But who says, when he looks upon the splendid marble buildings that adorn our cities, that all the noise, dust, and rubbish which obstructed the sidewalks, while those buildings were rising, had better not have been made, even though the price of unbroken neatness and order had been the perpetual continuance of the old, rat-riddled shanties, which were once where those palaces now stand?

New England is the right arm of the States, and Boston is the hand of that arm.

That arm is now outstretched, and that mighty

hand is clenched to give a death-blow to slavery. I never felt so willing to drop my oars as now.

Who would *row* when he could go *by sailing?*

Here is a letter from a southern slaveholder, a woman, who has written to me, *me!* for advice as to how to get rid of the slaves in a way which shall make them free, and not utterly impoverish herself.

When southern slaveholders write to me on such a subject as this, then I say it is not hard for us to believe that the millennium *is* drawing nigh.

To have God and the things of eternity consciously always in mind is impossible.

There is no provision, either in nature or grace, for such a state of things.

But to have him in our hearts, as the governing power of our lives, and to carry our love for him, consciously and unconsciously, as a mother carries the love of her first-born child, is what is our privilege and our duty to do, and our only safety. The mother thinks of ten thousand things which, for the time, *must* crowd her babe out of her mind; but never does she get free of the influence that her love for him has over her. We must make these natural loves our teachers of how we are to be filled with the love of God. We may go up by them till we are far, far above them in regard to what we feel for him, who has all loves in himself; but we never need to attempt impossibilities, for he will have no such worship. Remember grace is only *nature blossomed out;* it is no new thing grafted in upon nature, but nature won and warmed into its *true* growth; that for which the God of nature made it. A Christian is one brought back to true growing. Educate your children aright, inure them to hardness. Make them to be like the willow tree, that when broken from the parent stem, they may immediately root themselves wherever they strike ground, and bravely flourish on their own responsibility, instead of being forever grafting themselves on your old trunk and limbs. Don't make women of your sons; for thus would they have all woman's weakness, without her regal excellence.

A woman *made of a woman* is God's noblest work; but a woman made of *a man* is his meanest one.

THERE is no religion in the Bible—I hope if there are any reporters here, that they will wait until I finish my sentence before they run to the —— paper—any more than there is a road upon the guide-board. The Bible is the rule, the direc tion, by which man is to work out his own salvation, as the guide-board is the direction by which he is to walk out his journey. Religion is *in the man*, or it is not anywhere.

Religion should not be used as calking, something to stuff into the cracks and crevices of a man's life; but it should be regarded and used as the very warp and woof of life.

When all goes smoothly, men imagine themselves fully equal to driving their own team; but when their affairs begin to run away with them, they cry out quick enough, "Where's God? where's God?"

It ought to grow more and more easy to Christians to do right, until at last the acts that *were* sore self-denial become a pleasure.

When this has come to pass do not be frightened, and begin to doubt your piety. Be glad and grateful, for your graces are growing ripe.

What was once sour and bitter has become sweet and agreeable.

When you first entered the Christian path, you found it hard to do those things as conscience commanded, and you were often tempted to cry out:

"Thy paths are *not* the paths of peace, O God!"

You were as children who, hearing their father discourse of the rare and luscious apples that his orchard yielded, straightway ran thither, expecting, though it was in the early summer, to be able to judge of the flavor of the fruit. Biting into it, they cry with wry features, spitting and casting the apples to the ground. "Is *this* the perfumed, saccharine flavor our father talks of? We want no more of it."

The miser, when converted, finds that he must be a miser no more. He sees, perhaps, that duty requires him to give fifty dollars to a poor man. He wishes that twenty-five would do; but it *won't* do. He knows that. He puts his hand into his pocket and—considers. He tries to go away without giving the sum.

"Do it—do it," growls conscience from within.

The man casts down the money hastily, and runs away.

That was a victory, but a hard and painful one; and the miser finds himself put through years of just such discipline, until at last he is a miser no more.

Giving has become a blessing and a *pleasure* to his heart. Shall he now say, dolefully? "I *fear* I am not a true Christian. I cannot see that I carry any cross, or deny myself any, as once I did. Why, I remember when it was like crucifixion to give away five dollars. But I overcame nature and gave it, and then I had sure evidence that the root of the matter was in me. But now—oh! I'm so much at ease now, something must certainly be wrong; nothing seems to try me."

Why, man, your graces are growing fully ripe; or take another figure.

It is a great trick among the boys to ferule each other in order to harden their palms preparatory to blows thereon from the teacher.

It's a good thing sometimes to have the palms hardened. Yours have been hardened so that giving does not hurt them now.

THERE are localities where the gnats, flies, and mosquitoes are so thick that a man cannot see for them. They swarm about his head and eyes in such blinding numbers that it is utterly in vain to try to seek for anything upon the ground.

Thus, I think, it is with the Bible. It has been so beswarmed by commentators that it is next to impossible to think of a text without instantly hearing the buzz, buzz, buzz, of five hundred constructions and explanations, each one of which is further from being any help than the others are.

Our real commentators are our strongest traits of character; and usually, we come out of the Bible with such of its texts sticking to us as our idiosyncrasies attract.

The texts we least need are the ones we like best, and remember longest. A kind-hearted, *lazy* man will remember "Blessed are the merciful," long after he has forgotten the injunction to be "diligent in business."

Health underlies all there is of a man. I think a man ill-bodied cannot think healthily. It would surprise people to see how many things which have shaken the world with controversy, and burdened it with error, had their origin in indigestion. It is humbling, but it is true, that the action of the mind depends upon the state of the sinews and the blood. To be sure, there have been cases in which from a diseased body the mind has shone out strong and good, triumphant over fleshly ill; but these are not the rule. No man would think of going into battle with a handful of unarmed men, because such have won victories; or of going to sea in an unrigged ship because dismasted and dismantled vessels have come safely into port. Health is a duty. If a man would carry his mind aright, and have it work with *power*, let him seek to be healthy.

Christians all want to have graces, but they are not so willing to take what is necessary in order to obtain them. The pale think it a fine thing to be painted—all the lovely flowers and gay colors so skillfully laid on by the cunning hand of the artist; but when it comes to being daubed all over with some dark substance, when the very gold that is upon them becomes as black as ink; when they are thrust into the heated furnace, how then? how *then?*

Christians are like vases, they must pass through the fire ere they can shine. And often the very furnace and the flame which they call destruction, is only burning *in* the graces which are to be their everlasting beauty and glory.

Not so much is it *much* working as it is *easy* working, which tells. If a man only knows how to use himself, if he use all his faculties in due measure, he will scarce ever tire. Most men use but very few of their faculties. They are like a man who owns a tower in which are thirty bells; but he never attends to them. By and by there comes a day on which he would rejoice, and he goes to ring his bells. He draws this rope and that, but there is no response, or only a jingle now and then, from some cracked and rusty bell.

At last, from one great, hoarse throat, at the

top of the tower, comes crashing out a heavy sound.

That bell is the only one of the whole thirty that will ring.

Or, men are like houses, *built* very high, but which the owner had no means of *furnishing* higher than the first story—and there he lives, his upper chambers all going to rack and ruin. Or they are like ships well freighted and furnished, when they started out from port, but which, when they near their other harbor, have nothing left of them but their hull. They have made fuel of everything within themselves. They are self-consumed.

A MAN'S worth should be reckoned by what he is, not by what he has.

A WISE man is one that knows how to turn to good account the knowledge which he has. *He* is not wise who has mastered all languages, all sciences, if he lacks the ability to *use* this knowledge. *He is only stuffed.*

THE man who tries to cut himself and square his conduct merely by the outward pattern of morality, is as the artist who, instead of studying his art from the boundless and glorious pictures God has painted on the earth and in the sky, goes into some dim gallery, and pores over what hangs there until he can badly imitate the stiff drapery, uncouth figures, inhuman adults, and monstrous pumpkin-headed children, that the canvas before him exhibits. Ha! you love to laugh at the artists; but what do you think the angels do at *you*, who prostitute not merely your fingers and imaginations, but your whole spiritual nature, to the work of making, not bad pictures, but bad, incomplete, poverty-stricken men. "Is not morality good, as far as it goes?" say you. "Yes, certainly, *as far as it goes*." "Isn't *my* cable as good as yours, as far as it goes?" says the sailor who has a short cable to him who has one very long. "Yes," says the other, "as far as it goes; but what of that, when it won't go within fifty fathoms of bottom." And of what use, oh, moralist, is your cable, when it will not go within fifty fathoms of the place where it can take hold upon the soul's anchorage?

I DON'T blame a man for not understanding the mysteries of God any more than I should blame one who was standing in the Atlantic Ocean for saying, "I can't."

"Can't *what?*"

"I *cannot*."

"Not what?"

"I've been in ankle deep, and knee deep, and thigh deep; I've been in all over, and it's no use; I never can wade across the Atlantic Ocean."

"Of course you can't—nobody told you to. What did you try for? God never meant to have you do it, or he would have made it more shallow."

Just in this way do men act in regard to doctrines. They go out a little way on election, and back they come, shaking their heads, and saying, "It's very mysterious; I can't understand it." Then they try free agency, then decrees, etc., but they have no better success with them. Well, what of it? Man, by all his searching, cannot find out God. I am not ashamed to say that I do not understand his mysteries. I believe that what he says is true, if I cannot reconcile it. My own consciousness agrees with the most seemingly contradictory passages concerning free will and sovereignty. I know that I *am* free, that by my own choice I perform moral acts. That with me lies the power of sinning or refraining from sin, and yet when I go forth with my most buoyant sense of freedom to think and act, I am conscious of influences, of barriers which say, "Thus far, and no further."

I feel in my very nature that I am free, and yet that I do not direct my own steps, nor appoint my own bounds. I cannot reconcile this. I know it; and there it must rest.

God does us no violence. He uses us through the very nature which he gave to us, and through our free will.

The mulberry leaves are stripped from the tree, and the food which they make for the worm acts upon it according to its own nature. As their nature dictates, the worms spin their cocoons and sleep in them.

Then, when the little spinners have been despoiled, the loom is made and the silk is woven and stamped by the skill of man. Everything has been used according to its nature in the construction of the silk.

And the web which God is weaving, and the pattern with which he will mark it, will all be done in the same way.

The whole plan is in his mind now, and it will result as he intends, but only through the free action of the nature he has given to man. His plan embraced this idea from the very beginning of things, and every contingency is provided for in the eternal mind.

A *man* is better than a peer, a prince, or a king.

Some ministers are forever hammering out doctrines, making ploughs with which they do no work after they *are* made.

Now *I* make ploughs; but when I have finished them, I don't lay them away to be taken out and re-beaten the next year.

No; my business is to put handles in my plough, and then to fasten to it a team strong as eternity, and then to force it deep, deep into the soil, and rip, rip, rip, ousting the vermin, scattering the moles and nibbling mice, and making broad furrows, in which I may sow seed.

Doctrinal furrows are good for nothing unless they are planted, and doctrines should not be preached so high that they are above the head of everybody who walks on the ground.

The passions never keep Lent, they are always holding Carnival.

Each living man bears a relation to his whole race. His having lived will never cease to be felt throughout the universe. No man *can* live unto himself. We own each other, and God owns us all. A man never stands alone unrelated to anything; but his closest relation is always to his Creator.

A willow tree may stand far from the banks of

the stream, and with no apparent support, except from the ground about its trunk. But what are its roots doing? Down burrowing amid the rocks—forcing a way through the earth, seeking for openings—pushing whithersoever is the smell of moist soil—diving to the level of the cool well, and drinking deep of its nourishing waters, shooting out by the brookside, many, many rods away, till its banks are fringed like a shawl, seeking everywhere for the nutriment which gives life to the tree above them, is what the roots are doing; and man is like a tree, only *his* roots shoot upward as well as downward, and his firmest tie is to the heart of God, as his surest and best supply is from thence.

Who then can say, "I am mine own; I stand alone uninfluenced and uninfluencing."

There is little hope of ever uniting men on doctrines or ordinances.

I think I can see in the New Testament authority for Episcopacy, for Presbyterianism, and for Congregationalism. To me it seems, therefore, that the Apostle's idea was that the churches should be governed according to their necessities, taking one form, or another, as was best suited to them.

The only ground on which all Christians can have perfect union is the ground of *love*.

Why, a little while ago they gathered themselves together from the four corners of the earth to form one great Christian union; and the very first thing they did after they were assembled, was to disfranchise the whole band of Quakers—among whom God has his saints and angels, if he has any on earth. May they not have been permitted to present to the world this absurd spectacle for the purpose of showing the impossibility of Christians uniting on mere grounds of opinion. Love is the *only* fusing power in the universe—all *may* meet there.

Three naturalists once went into the woods to find a nightingale's nest. When they had found it, each took from his pocket his favorite work on ornithology and began to describe the looks and the size of the nightingale that was not there. All gave a different description, and they quarrelled over the empty nest, and tore each other's books, and made a great noise. But now from the thicket where she had been resting, the bird began to pour a flood of song. The disputers stopped to listen. The very leaves quiver in the gush of melody—the waves of air are moved—the forest is bathed in music as in a flood. When a hush falls around them—for the song is done, the men straightway shut their books and go home.

Men read about God, and his character, and

they try to think about it, and undertake to de scribe it, and finally they get to quarrelling about what none of them at all understand. But sometimes when the truth shines out clearly on them, they forget all their supposed wisdom, and in silence go their ways to love and to adore.

SUPPOSE that I knew a body of men conspicuous for their faith, hope, love, gentleness, generosity, etc., but before I gave them my confidence I wanted to dig down a little deeper than practical life, and I said, "My dear sirs, what are your ideas concerning the Trinity?"

"Well," they reply, "we don't know much about that. In fact, we have no theory in regard, to it."

I then question them in regard to the "perseverance of saints."

"We have all been so busy trying to persevere that we haven't had time to study upon the doctrine," is the answer. And so on to the end of the doctrines.

Then, in order to be orthodox, I should have to shake my head at them and say;

"You *may* escape into heaven, so as by fire; but I don't know, I don't know—I will pray for you."

"Sound doctrine," says Orthodoxy, "is the foundation of religion." No such thing—Jesus Christ is the foundation of religion. Doctrine is the most delusive goblin that ever existed, when it is in the hands of certain men. They frame a form for Truth, and when she has outgrown and forsaken that form they stuff it with doctrine and bid men cling to the old shell and let the living spirit escape them.

I THINK that it is the sense of right and wrong that marks the line between man and the brutes. I'm sure I've seen some dogs that had more sense of right and wrong than some men have; and I think when you get down so low that this sense is wanting, you have come to beings that are neither human nor accountable, be their form what it may. But at least it is dark and twilight exploring in this direction.

THE ministry is inclined to think that a truth has no chance at all with refined and educated men, unless it have a refined dress. Now, although it is true that such men do look for what shall accord with their delicate and elevated tastes, and although even the truth of God is better if presented in chaste and elegant language, there are always, in every man's heart, great cords underlying all these lighter desires, which will answer instantly and powerfully to the touches of *feeling*—even though it be rudely expressed. When a man overflows, and in his efforts to express himself knocks his language in all directions, his honest, earnest, outright, downright feeling is the power which moves. It would be mightier were it well expressed, but the *feeling* is the thing after all; and when a man holds back feeling until it chokes in the sand, that he may present a correct and refined discourse, he *betrays Christ to rhetoric.*

When Paul said he was determined to know nothing but Christ and him crucified, he was upon this same theme. He was telling the people that he was not going to tickle their ears with fine, smooth periods. He said: "My power upon you shall not be in my refined and elegant language, in my persuasive eloquence. It will not be in me *at all,* but in my moving subject, Christ and him crucified. He was going to throw over them no lasso of ensnaring art; he would declare to them the plain truth in words that all could understand and feel. Paul meant no such thing as ministers mean now-a-days, when they make this declaration. *He* did not mean by it that he should shun all touching upon the things on which duty called him to speak out boldly, that he should meddle with nothing that could offend the sinning public, but talk perpetually of Christ and him crucified, without making this his lever to heave from their foundations the evils of the world. Such talk is nonsense, in the pulpit or out of it—consummate nonsense.

WERE angry and unkind words and thoughts like thunder and lightning, we should have one unending storm, sweeping round and round the whole earth.

WERE one to ask me in which direction I think man strongest, I should say, in his capacity to hate.

I THINK that Scripture passages are like wayside flowers. We have seen them all our lives, and therefore do not know or feel their beauty; or they are like the beautiful creations of art that are in old cathedrals, covered by the dirt and moss of ages. Men go by them and do not know that they have passed forms that gave expression to the thoughts of ancient masters. No man cares for them, or cleans them, until by and by some enthusiastic Ruskin comes along and does it, and then 'tis seen that the things which all their life long they have thought homely, are beautiful beyond description.

What an idea of God's prodigality must have

been in Paul's mind when he thus struggled to express himself: "unto him who is able to do for you exceeding abundantly more than ye can ask or think." And *this* was his view of his master's character when he was in prison, and when, apparently, affairs with the church were desperate. This view he held up in the sky for Christians to steer by. Such abundance belonged to God, and God was theirs. Abundance is a relative word. A shepherd would not consider that abundance for him which might be so for a wayfarer. What would be abundance for a nomad would not do for the supply of the settled farmer, and the farmer's abundance would be a scant portion for the merchant. A petty prince of a German province would require far more than the abundance of the merchant to support his state, yet what would make his coronet resplendent would be but a trifle in that of the Russian czar. When from these we look up to heaven, and try to imagine what that can be which *Infinity* names abundance—"more than ye can ask or think"—we are bewildered, and give up in despair. In the hours when the spirit wafts our souls upward as the wind sometimes lifts a bird, aiding its flight, we wish, and think, and ask such things, as afterwards we wonder how we dared to mention; we cannot believe ourselves that we ever soared so high as we yet are conscious of having done. When the heart yearns for ourselves, or for others, we ask such blessings as we almost fear are presumptuous. But even a mother's heart, deep as the eternal wells, when in her closet she kneels amid the sound of groans, and the plashing of falling tears, to pray for her wandering child; even the prayers of martyrs, in their utmost agony, when their words swept like the Amazon, and were yet but bubbles on the sea of feeling that was beneath, were shallow and poverty-struck compared to what he will give to each one who loves him. Why, look at the beginning; when a child is sent to earth, what preparation of soft quilted fabric, of all delicate and curiously-wrought garments, scented with sweetest perfumes, is made for the little pilgrim of love! But what is all this to the expense and lavish outfit of earth, the cradle of man's infancy? See how its furniture is wrought. One fragrant bank, could he, in his whole lifetime, produce such a one, would render an artist immortal.

God has quilted the earth with beauty, and combed the hair of ten million flowers and reeds over its verdant banks. No emperor's child was ever rocked in such a cradle.

Does the mother lavish less love upon her child as it grows in stature and capacity? And shall God do less lovingly than those whose hearts he made and filled with love from his own heart?

Some men think of God as of one sitting like a thunderstorm in the sky. They know that there is no safety but in going to him, but they apprehend a great deal of danger even in that.

They approach him under an umbrella of excuses, and have, here and there, a covert under which to dodge, if they think a bolt is coming. They forget who Christ meant by the "Father" of the prodigal Son; and they lose all the encouragement that he meant for repentant sinners, when he represented God as in such a hurry to welcome him who had returned that he *ran to meet him* while he was yet *a great way off*, and would not for kisses let him tell *half* his shame and sorrow. Some say 'tis dangerous to say too much of God's love. Men take advantage of it, and become universalists. They say: "Preach justice for bread; let mercy be cake."

The Bible is the centre jewel of which creation is the setting.

Were the office of deacon rotary in *all* churches, as it is in ours, we should not see the absurd spectacle of deacons trying to turn away a minister because he had removed deacons who deserved removal—thus trying to make the higher office subservient to the lower.

While I heartily despise the whole crew of religionists—the scribes, pharisees, and learned dunces, of our Saviour's time, who saw the most wonderful things passing about them, and did not know it, I don't want to be caught playing the same fool's part, in respect to what God is working in *our* land and times.

I want to praise God, and take part in helping it along.

The most of everything is that which is unexpressed.

Words are but little bubbles thrown up to express what lies below, forever inexpressible.

Ecclesiasticism has always been the devil's cloak under which to work evil.

I think that every church should have charge, as one of its indirect duties, growing out of its more peculiar and important ones, of the physical interests of its members and their families—and instruction in regard to bodily training, and to the preservation of health, should be provided for all the people. Religion would gain wonderfully by the regeneration of the *body*.

There is not a street in Brooklyn where I could not point you out heroic women before whom the chronicled deeds of the historic dames of the ancient world would blush for very shame of their own insignificance. The world has advanced. Heroic deeds have become so common that they pass unnoticed.

When you have repented of your wrong and turned from it—no matter with how little feeling, for who feels enough to forsake his sin feels sufficiently, and the man that is scourged like a hound by feeling is none the better for more than it took to turn him—*you are not to trouble yourself about it any more.*

God forgets your sin when he forgives it. So may, so ought *you.*

Great sinners who have offended against honesty and purity, when they are converted, sometimes try to keep their former sins up before them; lest, unaware, they who had been so awfully wicked, should forget it, and enjoy themselves.

They check every pleasurable emotion by the reflection: "Ah! think, think, what it was that you did. You are not worthy to laugh and be glad."

True; they are not worthy. Nor is any one, in and of himself; but I care not what their sins may have been, when they are forgiven of God, they should be cast into the depths of the sea, and remembered no more forever.

The man that keeps tormenting himself by the memory of repented and forsaken sins, *is a fool*—a fool! To repent and forsake sin is sufficient, when there is no way of making an atonement; but if there *is* a way, the atonement must be made, or you may be sure that your repentance is a sham, and will never be accepted.

MEN confess everything but their own besetting sins. They steer quite clear of these. Who ever heard a man say: "O Lord! I am as proud as Satan—humble me;" or, "O Lord! I am so mean and stingy, that 'tis only with great pain that I can unclose my fists. Make me generous."

SUPPOSE I were to set out on a pilgrimage to Jerusalem, and before I started were to go to Brown Brothers & Co., and obtain letters of credit for the cities of London, Jericho, etc. Then, with these papers which a child might destroy, which would be but ashes in the teeth of flame, which a thousand chances might take from me, I should go on with confidence and cheer, saying to myself, "As soon as I come to London I shall be in funds.

I have a letter in my pocket from Brown Brothers & Co., which will give me five hundred dollars there; and in the other cities to which I am bound I shall find similar supplies, all at my command, through the agency of these magic papers and pen strokes of these enterprising men." But, suppose that instead of this confidence I were to sit down on shipboard, and go to tormenting myself in this fashion: "Now, what *am* I to do when I get to London? I have no money, and how do I *know* that these bits of paper which I have with me mean anything, or will amount to anything? What shall I do? I am afraid I shall starve in the strange city to which I am going." I should be a fool, you say; but should I be *half* the fool that that man is who, bearing the letters of credit of the Eternal God, yet goes fearing all his way, cast down and doubting whether he shall ever get safe through his journey? No fire, no violence, nor any chance, can destroy the checks of the Lord. When he says: "I will never leave thee, nor forsake thee," and "my grace shall be sufficient for thee," believe it; and no longer dishonor your God by withholding from him the confidence which you freely accord to Brown Brothers & Co.

The years! how they have passed. They are gone as clouds go, on a summer day. They came, they grew, they rolled full-orbed; they waned, they died, and their story is told.

Years that wrought upon us, in thought and deed, with the force and power of eternity; years, whose marks we shall carry forever, were dissolved like the dew, and their work is finished.

And the days have gone. With a gentle swell comes their knell backward to us, over the ocean. Slipped from their cables, the bright days glide one by one away from us, drifting with airy speed over the shoreless tide, beating faint, sweet measures as they recede from our longing view. We may stand long upon the shore, and call them; but they will not return; they are ours no more.

Awful is the dirge of years. It is an anthem too solemn and grand for tears; but we may weep for the dying days. Faintly they sigh to us of by-gone hours, of moments fragrant with all human joys, of friends and familiars, whose smiles at morning cheered our way, but whose faces at evening were covered; for still as life lengthens the shadows fall, and the *past* is forever gathering treasures.

The hopes that are born, that grow ripe and die, float out, as the days, on the ebbing tide.

Gorgeous and rich are the shrines in many lands, but what temple was ever builded as some days are. Marvellous fancies, deeds, in whose doing the heart grows strong, thoughts too mighty for words, feelings that are deeper than the utmost depths of thought; *these* are the material out of which days are built, and no Vatican or cathedral walls ever blazed with such glories of picture as are often painted on single days.

As they move softly towards the far horizon, how do our hearts follow, with yearning love, the motions of the parting days! We would hold them back, but we cannot, and in the golden sunset the bright days sink. And with them how many that we loved depart. Loved! nay, *love*, for the love remains to shine on the memory of those who have left us, like the lamps that are kept burning in sepulchres.

Two weeks ago I told you that three thousand dollars had got to be raised to pay for the repairs of this house.

The plates were sent round, and about six hundred dollars were raised.

I was heartily ashamed, and have not got over it yet. Last week the trustees came, and asked me if I would name the matter again, and I said: "No, I will *not*." But this week, upon their renewed application, I have consented to speak once more. If this don't do, you may pay your debt how you can; for I will never mention it again. I'm not going to be a pump to be thrust into men's pockets to force up what ought to come up freely.

When the surgeon comes to a place where he must cut, he had better *cut.* For more than a year I've seen that our plate-collections grew meaner and meaner. I didn't want to face you with such things as I've got to say to-day, and I put it off as long as I could. Now I shall speak plainly once for all, not having the face to bring the matter up again. This debt has got to be paid, and will you meet it honorably, and pay it like men, or will you let it drip, drip, drip out of you reluctantly, a few dollars at a time? You can take your choice. I'm not going to try to drill money out of you as I would drill stones. Our lecture-room holds about three hundred people, and we collect from thirty to eighty dollars there every time we pass the plate. Our best Christians attend the weekly meetings, and they are always the most generous. In this congregation, that numbers over three thousand, we don't average *one cent per head* in our collections.

While there are, thank God, many of his poor among us, who cannot give him a shilling without making a difference in all their arrangements for a whole week, there are hundreds of men here who ought to be ashamed *ever* to give anything but gold, or, at least a bill. And they *are* ashamed to do it. Don't they, when the plate approaches, and they have put their fingers in their pockets and selected a quarter—the smoothest one that they can find—use admirable tact and skill in conveying it to the plate, so that no one shall see what they give? Pious souls! they don't allow their left hand to know what their right hand doeth. If they have two bills, one good, one broken, they'll generally give the broken one to the Lord. The amount of meanness among respectable people is appalling. One needs to take a solar microscope in order to see some men. I'm willing to give my share, to *do* whatever the trustees desire; I shall *say* no more.

I WOULD not, for the world, bring up a child to have that horror of death which hung over my own childhood.

I think I never came nearer swooning than when I heard of the death of one of my young companions. I walked in a shadow for two days, hardly able to tell whether I was in the body or out of it.

The thought of death was to me awful beyond description. The toll of the funeral bell would cheat me out of my most desired meal. To my imagination its stroke was thus: "Death! hell! damnation!" Our children should be taught that a funeral is the nearest place to heaven; instead of which, I think, they oftener feel it to be the nearest place there is on earth to hell.

I do not say what death should be to the impenitent—it is a pass at which no mistake can be rectified—let all beware how they come up to it; but I say this, that to the Christian, and to the little child, it is the best and most joyful thing that life leads to—the portal into everlasting blessedness; and thus it should always be represented.

Tell your child when, after long imprisonment in school, he one day hears his father at the gate, come to take him home, and while his young heart shakes his whole frame in nervous ecstasy, that this is like what dying is, but not half as much, or half as joyful. Death is vacation. God comes to take us from this old, rolling academy, a good school, but a hard one, and bear us home with him. Then, should the house be draped with signs of woe, as if it were plague-smitten?

YOUNG men, you come here to get good advice; now hear it. I tell you there is nothing in the world so profitable as are lying and stealing—I should not like to drop down now, before I finished this sentence—so profitable in the beginning, but so sure to be hit by God's lightning at the end.

You can gain fast, but you will lose fearfully and rapidly.

When suspicion begins to touch you the end is near.

And when that time comes, if the rocks would fall from their everlasting beds and crush you and hide you, it would be unutterable mercy, compared with the burden of shame and contempt that you must bear.

My heart is towards the young yet. Only when I look in the glass and see how the grey hairs are coming on my head, do I know that I am growing old. By the beating of my heart I should never know it. My heart is towards the young yet. Would that I *could* warn them so that they would heed; but they hear me, and they will go away and remember naught. They will follow *their* footsteps who are as *sure* to topple and go down to ruin as the sun is to rise and shine.

There are men in both these cities, whose names I could call, on whom the eyes of those just entering the work of life are fixed for imitation, but whose end is damnation.

See how it is with many corrupt public men. One lately died in New England. They prosper for a time. Then sink into obscurity, and after a while there is a little paragraph in the paper—"Such a one is *dead*." That is all that men see.

But could they look into the man, and see his mental history for his last few years; could they see the disappointed hopes, the defeated plans, the chagrins, the mortifications; see all the vermin that haunted the secret chambers of that abused house; the evil thoughts, the wicked wishes that ran in and out, like rats and reptiles in old, dilapidated and gipsy-haunted fortresses, see the man stranded, high and dry, dropping, dropping, dropping; until at last the rotten thing sunk entirely and fell into utter corruption, and the papers said, "He is dead," they would not be so eager so follow his steps, nor to dare his end. A snake can lap itself around till it inserts its tail into its mouth; if I had power to ring life thus, and make its ends meet, I would save many; but the sweet comes first, and men will not believe in the bitter until it is too late.

The lad tries being industrious for a week, and because he don't see immediate good results he gives up the effort. He tries dishonesty, and the gain is in his hands at once; so he calls evil, good; forgetting that evil is always ready grown, and yields its *pleasant* fruit at once. That's the best he will ever have from it; afterwards it grows worse and worse continually.

Good is ungrown and imperfect in this life, and often its fruit is very long in ripening. Evil is the plump, round egg; Good, the callow and unfledged bird, unshapely, helpless, and that cannot even peep with any strength.

But by and by the true nature of each will appear. Suppose a man were to go out and sow radish seed and acorns at the same time. In a few weeks he goes to see how they do.

"Oh!" he says, "radishes are a great deal better for timber than oak is. Here I sowed my seed a month or more ago, and the acorns haven't even sprouted, while the radishes are as big as my wrist."

You plant your evil, and it springs up like radishes, when your good has not even sprouted. A man says, "I told the truth all last week, even many times to my own hurt, and I got into a great deal of trouble by it. This week I've told lies all the week, and I can see that there has been much advantage to me in it." Nobody thinks indiscriminate lying would be good, but each man thinks that if everybody else would speak truth, *he* should, then, be a great gainer by lying.

Often it *does* look to us as it looked to the psalmist himself, that the way to be prosperous and happy is to be bad, and the way to be miserable is to be good. But the truth is not so.

God works upon man by means of all events, all natural influences. The mere naturalist goes abroad and says, "Don't tell me that I'm what God makes me. I'm what my parents make me, what natural law makes me, what social influences make me. I'm the child of ten thousand different influences." The pious dreamer says, "I am fashioned by God;" he jumps all intervening causes, as entirely unworthy of notice. As usual, extremes meet in a common blunder. God does not work directly on man, save in exceptional cases. Where a man was born and how he is nurtured and taught, make him; but all the influences that play upon him are ordained of God. Man is as an instrument of music whose key board is so broad that a hundred hands may play upon it, and each player execute different tunes. Many and diverse influences operate at once upon the mind of man, and although the *direction* in which he was set at his birth will have something, perhaps much, to do with what he becomes, his native tendencies will be modified by ten thousand circumstances. The natural things which touch the man are all under the control of the Supernal Power.

CHILDREN think much more and much more deeply than we are aware, upon religious subjects. I remember that I was seriously exercised upon the doctrines of election, free-agency, etc., by the time that I was eight years old. I was brought up on doctrine. The things that most influence children are *acted* things; not things that are said.

I don't remember to have been affected by any sermon until I was more than thirteen years old. But the prayer and talking meetings were the ones. I used to be convicted there; and I would go about trying to be "pricked in the heart." I had got that figure and so tried to prick myself. I wanted to be taken up by some resistless wind of conviction, and to be made to suffer such agonies about my sinful state as I had heard others tell of; for I thought that right after that would follow conversion, and I should be safe.

I don't think fear has much really good influence upon children—a *powerful* influence it certainly does have. I remember once we children were all called together into our kitchen—which we thought the best room in the house; its windows looked out upon trees and flowers, and its door, when opened, revealed the long line of road along which we always made haste to run as soon as we could gain our freedom. We were called into the kitchen to be talked to by a minister who was staying at my father's. He told us how wicked boys and girls were by nature, and what an awful end was before them if they never repented. He told us the story of one wicked boy who saw the devil coming after him. The idea almost froze our young blood with horror, and we resolved with all our might to be good, that such a fate might not befall us. But as for myself I don't think that talk ever did me one particle of good; on the contrary, I believe I never did cut up so bad any one week as I did that week, spite of all my efforts to stop myself by thoughts of that dreadful story, and of how I should feel to see the devil coming up the road after *me*.

I remember that one Sunday morning, as soon as I awoke, I began to play, picking the cotton out of the quilt, and rolling it into balls to throw at my brother. Suddenly came the thought "You wicked boy! to begin the Sabbath by playing."

At once I was condemned, and ducked beneath the bed-clothes lest something dreadful should catch me. There I lay quietly five minutes, as long as I ever kept still.

There came a woman to live with us—Aunty Chandler we were taught to call her; she became my fast friend, and used to beg me off from whippings. There was a tree whose apples used to get me up and out early in the morning. I was often whipped for stealing them; but whippings used to make me very brave. One morning, just as I was stealing out to go for the apples, Aunty Chandler stopped me: "Oh! Henry," she said, tears rolling down her face, "I cannot bear to have you whipped so; why *will* you go and get those apples?"

This was a new idea. It had never struck me that Aunty C. got the whippings on her heart. After that there were not ropes enough in old Connecticut to draw my young feet to that tree.

In those days people used to get together and pray and make a solemn time of it when a train of emigrants were about to start for Ohio. It was almost as if they were to start for another world. Well do I remember the long lines of white-covered wagons that used to wind through Litchfield, and I used to run into the house and hide under the table that they might not steal and carry me off. Well, the time came when Aunty Chandler went away in one of those slow-moving trains. I shall never forget it. I thought I was near the end of *my* gospel when she went. Her life was strong in its good influence upon me. Next came a negro servant. He was my next evangelist. I used to watch him in the field, and in the house, and even now, with my mature reflection, I cannot remember ever to have seen him do a wrong act. As I worked beside him in the field, he used to tell me his experience, and where he learned this and that hymn; and then he would sing as only the African can sing, and I used to wish that I could have such religion as that negro enjoyed. When we went to bed—he and I slept in the same garret, he in one corner and I in the other; some people would think it a dreadful thing to have to share a garret with a negro—when we went to bed he used to pile his pillows up behind him so that he could *lie sitting up*, take his hymn-book, fasten his candle up somewhere so that he could see, and commence having a regular good time. He would sing hymn after hymn with such relish and enjoyment, the big tears frequently rolling down his dark face, that I used to be cut to the heart with remorse, that I, a minister's son, brought up with every advantage, should be so much worse than a poor negro. I would lie there and pretend to be asleep, while all the time —— —— was singing right at my conscience, and I was crying heartily to hear him. Oh! how glad I should have been could I have changed places with that poor negro serving-man, if it hadn't been for cheating him. I think that *lived*, *acted out* religion does more good to children than all the talking that can be done, though talking certainly should not be omitted. That African did me more good than all the ministers that ever came to my father's house.

The infidelity of the last twenty-five years has been that which has sought to emasculate religion, by separating it from practical life, and lifting it so far above everybody's daily and familiar use, that they might as well be without it. The pretence is, that religion is too sacred to be rendered useful in common matters. Over the church doors men write: "Religion is religion;" and over the store door: "Business is business." And the church says to business: "Don't you come in here;" and the store says to religion: "Don't *you* come in *here*."

Man rejects the interference of the higher law in his business as an impertinence. But when Sunday comes, he says: "We've had enough of business all the week; now let us have the blessed Gospel."

And the minister must confine himself to "Christ and him crucified." He mustn't mention love to God and man shown in business transactions, for he must preach the Gospel; he mustn't exhort to temperance, for he must preach the Gospel; he mustn't preach of justice, purity, and humanity, for he must preach *the Gospel.*

Why, if men catch "the higher law" on 'change, or in the street, they hoot at it, they chase it, they hit it, and drive it from among them, crying out: "Here is this higher law escaped out of the church, and out of the Sunday."

The worst spectacle which this country now presents is not, I think, the governmental or political corruptions, though these are enormous; but it is that of a religious body, like the one in New

York, utterly refusing to open its mouth against the blackest iniquity of the age.

And for what, in the name of Heaven? What reason do they give for their strange silence? Why, because if it does speak against this sin it will not be allowed to preach the Gospel. If every sin were as powerful as is the sin of slavery, what would these preachers of the Gospel do? Keep silence in regard to them all, of course; for, according to their views, only the smaller and least powerful sins can be safely hit.

That ponderous body can bombard men bravely for using tobacco, but it can't say one word against selling men and women to raise it. It can spend itself and exert its tremendous machinery against the awful sin of the dancing of young men and maidens; but can't utter a sound when maidens are sold to prostitution, and young men are driven off, in chain-gangs, to the rice swamps of Georgia.

The use which I make of such men, is to point the young to them, and say: "There are men whom you must shun to resemble."

The worst stamp of Phariseeism was not in our Saviour's day. It has, after years of monstrous growth, exhibited itself in the nineteenth century.

THE Bible sets us an example of fashioning for ourselves a personal God to suit our need.

When I find Paul using figures to represent to himself God, as his wants required him, I know that I may do the same thing. When I want love, I may make God my tender and loving father, or sister, or mother. When I want pity, I may make him a being of unfailing and boundless pity. When I want courage, he is my lion; when I want light and cheer, he is my bright and morning star—my God alert, my sun, my bread, my wine. We may imagine him *everything* that is to us good and beautiful, tender and true, and know that we are not cheating ourselves by vain fancies, but have only touched the extreme outer edge of the ever-blessed reality. There may be dangers in this freedom and variety of our representation of our God; but there are dangers in all forms of our thought of him, and in none half so much as in having no realization of him at all, in considering him as an abstraction of all the omnis. Thinking of him thus, none can *ever love him*, or *walk with him*.

This everlasting twaddle of infidelity about fixed natural laws, is simple foolishness.

I should like to know, now, if *man* even has not as much power over natural laws, wherever they touch him, as natural laws have over him. True, God says to man, in one place, "Obey;" but in other places, he says: "Command!"

Nature can work roughly and coarsely in generalities; but she needs men's intellect and will to give effect to what she does.

Through hundreds and thousands of years she tried her hand at making apples, and they were but *crab-apples* at last.

Man said, "I will help you; and by his industry and wisdom, the sour, miserable fruit soon covered all the hills with luscious apples.

I have power over nature's laws to make them work for my own and my children's good. I can make the lightning my amanuensis and my messenger. I can make the sun himself my artist; but when did ever the unassisted sun paint a picture? Man whispers to him: "Come down here, and I will tell thee something that thou knowest not," and the sun obeys. "Go through there," says man, and the sun goes through, and finds himself painting pictures. I should like to see him try to do that alone. I can say to the sea, "Wait on my will," and it obeys me; to the stream: "Thou lazy thing, flow no longer down hill, but up," and it flows up. When I turn it into a machine, I say to the water, "Grind," and it grinds my food. Natural laws are God's horses, and he says to man: "Vault," and he who can ride them is their master. By working them according to their nature, we can make them to do a million things that they could *never* do without us. By obeying, we command. They are the blind giants which our will and wisdom guide. Is not this true? Have I perplexed you with metaphysics? Have I not rather showed you plain facts, which you can follow out to almost any extent?

Remember, the question between me and the infidel naturalist is not, "Does God disturb natural laws in order to answer the prayers of his people, or does he do violence to nature that he may do any man good?" but it is this: "Is it, or is it *not*, likely that he is able to do for those who call upon him and whom he loves as well as man can do by means of natural law for those dear to *him?*" In other words, "Is it likely that one who has given to his creatures such wonderful power over laws of his own creating, should be himself so bound and hampered by them that there should be with him no possibility of any modification of their working to suit circumstances? The idea is absurd, and they are fools who indulge it. That man who says and believes that there is no effect on God's feelings and actions by prayer, is not a Christian. I'd rather a man would do as Martin Luther did—lay down his hand on a promise and say to God, "Now, here is thy word, O! Lord! fulfill it to me, or I never will believe thee again, as long as I live." God will interfere and help us, no matter what laws we have broken. If we didn't break laws we shouldn't *need* his help; because we have broken, and do break them, he does help all who trust in him and even most of those that don't. When it is *proved* that praying alters nothing, I will say of the Bible, "It was a pleasant book; but it has passed."

Not all prayers are answered. When you ask for what would take away motive for exertion; when you ask for what you do not really need, or for what would hurt you, you will not, probably, get what you desire.

But when a man, out of his deep want, goes to God for a good gift which he is powerless to gain for himself, he shall have it. This is the seal. God is more willing to give good gifts unto them that ask him, than parents are to give good gifts unto their children. Do you believe *that?*

I do not fear science; I love it. I do not look with jealous eye upon it lest it cut off some of my ground. I accept all truth, when it is proved, no matter where it carries me; but I don't accept what every man calls truth, any more than I believe the tale of every beggar that comes to my door.

Infidels are working for God, though they do not

know it. They shake and rend his truths until they think that they have destroyed them, but they have only cleared them of the shuck. I think infidels are like swine that, going into a corn-field tear down the mighty grass, and crunch its leaves and ears, trampling into the earth all that they cannot eat. Then, they go out thinking that they have devoured or buried all the corn. Yes, they have buried it for resurrection; for from its grave it shall rise in tenfold glory, to wave all the more luxuriantly for that husbandry of hoof and snout. So is it with infidel swine in the corn-field of God's Word.

WHOEVER has been enabled to take hold upon another's interest in such a manner as to *give himself*, for the time being, for that other, and to feel that his friend's life is dearer than his own, has attained to one of the purest and highest states into which man on earth ever comes. And he should understand that a very high experience has been granted him.

To be lifted above temptations; never to have a wrong thought, or a wrong moving of the affections, is a very good thing, but it is not being so *Christ-like* as he is who bears upon his soul another's life—who suffers for him, yearns for him, would give his life to do him good. This is the very spirit of Christ Jesus, and *if we suffer* with him we shall also reign with him. And we *must* suffer with him, if we would reign with him. But now, the other truth which meets this. We have no business to be so linked with any other human being as that their destination shall be ours. All suffering more than that which makes us ready to do all in our power for their good, we must fight against. It can do only harm. We must have our best and dearest friends to know that our peace in God cannot be destroyed. Not husband nor wife, brother nor sister, nor friends have any right to cause rust and canker to enter our souls for them. *Who* shall separate us from the love of God? We must do all we can, and do it in a cheerful, winning way, so as not to repel and torment them, thus hindering the very thing we would hasten. But when we have done all we *must* wait God's time. This is what all those injunctions to patience mean. But there is another thought, "What if our friends should die?" You have no right to meddle with that, nor to try to settle the state of any one who *does* die. And, beside, do you not know that this necessity of seeing men go unprepared to death, was what the apostles, the prophets, yes, and Christ himself was obliged to look upon and bear? But remember, God's pity is for the time of trouble and distress. He is your tower—run into it, and be safe. I would not give two cents for a faith that wouldn't help me while I need help. Christ has offered to bear my burdens, and *he shall* have them. *Here* are my trials, temptations, and woes, not in heaven, and here is where I have most need of my Saviour.

No man is born into the full Christian character, any more than he is born into the character of a man when he comes into the world. A man at conversion is in the state of one who has just come into possession of an old homestead. He has the title and he can make for himself a beautiful home. But the dust, the dirt, and the cobwebs of years choke all the rooms, and must be cleared away. Many sills and beams are rotten and must be replaced by new ones. Chambers must be refitted, walls newly plastered, the whole roof must be searched over, and every leak stopped. There must be a thorough cleansing and repair before the mansion is habitable; and when all this is done 'tis only *an empty house* that the man has.

The same kind of thing that a man is, who has trained himself into freedom from wrong, without having become faithful in right deeds.

Now for a man's house he may buy carpets ready made; but there is no loom that will weave carpets for his heart, except the loom that is in himself. Furniture, beds, chairs, and tables, he may buy for his house, but rest and peace for his soul can only be worked out within his soul, and long labor it often proves. He may purchase paintings, whose voiceless language shall make eloquent his walls, and statues to grace niche and pedestal, and books to fill his many shelves, but the painter, the sculptor and the publisher for the man's mental house are all in his own heart.

We are all painting pictures in the dark. Oh! this painting in the dark! what is to be revealed when the light cometh? It is fearful.

I think that persons who are sincerely resolved to fashion themselves upon the pattern of Christ, but who can see no marks upon, or in themselves of their own success, are like artists painting in the dark, beautiful pictures which shall astonish them with their loveliness when the morning shines upon their work. Or, they are like flowers, talking together in the night, and saying: "We are not beautiful as we desire to be." They wished to be arrayed in gay colors, and to have jewels of dew upon their buds and leaves; but they answer mournfully to each other's questionings: "It is all darkness upon you; nothing can be seen." Then they hold up their heads, and stretch out their leaves; but a weight oppresses them, and again they droop, complaining that no brightness or beauty is given them. But all the while the night is distilling its gentle moisture on those unconscious flowers, and the very jewels for which they murmur and sigh, are gathering thickly on every leaf and stem. They are bathed in the dew of freshness and fragrance, and crowned with the most radiant gems. And by and by, the morning breaks, and the moment that the glorious sun rolls above the horizon, and floods, with his slant beams, the world, ten million flowers glisten and glow with jewels of such lustre as was never known in diamond from Golconda's mines, nor in any precious stone on monarch's brow.

Periodical excitements are normal to the human constitution. Our very life stands on this foundation. Sixteen hours' excitement and eight hours' stupor—sleep.

There is in the human soul "a common feeling," which, being roused and stimulated, renders it possible for men to do in one hour the ordinary work of ten. It is somewhere said, "God never works by periodical fits." But I can hardly think of an instance in which he works otherwise.

A man has a right to stimulate himself, for right purposes, in his lower, intermediate, and higher nature. It is needful that he should do so. All men recognize this need in regard to business, politics, social life—but if needful here, where the senses and even selfishness have much influence, how much *more* needful when we rise into the realm of moral and spiritual things! Revivals of religion are in strict accordance with natural law. They are not to supersede the regular, calm, organized action of the church, but to work with all this, as an occasional, especial power. Men are energized by the Holy Spirit, and made able to work rapidly. But when the excitement is worn out, let it go. Don't try to keep it up unnaturally, or by effort. All strong feeling must rest *quick.*

To men who object to this intensifying a work, or to repenting in a hurry and under excitement, it may be said, "See to it, then, that you take the first calm moments when the reaction arrives to become a Christian, or you will prove that these objections of yours are all mere excuses to escape conversion."

When men have a great stone to move, they first dig away all the earth around it, working moderately and taking care to reserve their strength. When the earth is removed, they apply their lever, and now all take hold. At the word, "Now heave, men, heave!" each man strains with nerve and sinew—he throws his whole strength into that moment's effort, and the stone is forced from its bed.

Now what if some man, just as the final effort were about to be made were to cry out, "Stop, men, stop! Have you reflected well on what you are about to do? Have you thought whether you will be able to keep on working all day at the rate you will work while upheaving that stone?"

What better than this is he who objects to being lifted up upon the spring tide of a revival, because he is afraid he cannot always afterwards live up to that mark.

He is not required to live so. It is not possible. His feelings should always be deep like the sea; but they should *not* always roll and swell like the sea's agitated waves.

There are seasons in which the social and the moral feelings should thus move and mount, and at such times becoming a Christian is much easier work than at others; and although there are many very good Christians born when all is calm, and there is no religious excitement about them, yet *I* like a revival-born Christian best; for he is apt to be more open-hearted and of more use.

Some say revivals cause a great deal of self-deception—quick conversions are not apt to be thorough. This might be a sensible remark among heathens who do not know the first principles of the Gospel; but in communities like ours, where from the very cradle men are taught all the head knowledge that they need, and where the question is simply one of the will, "Will you submit to the rule of Christ, renouncing the ways of wickedness, or will you not?" it's a mere quibble of unbelief. The New Testament pauses not a moment over such miserable arguments. "Repent and believe *now*," is its doctrine, and three thousand souls were added to the church in *one day*. The Lord recognized the fact that many tares would be gathered in with the wheat; but he never, on that account, sanctioned people to *wait to be soundly converted*. "Let both grow together till the harvest," is his command.

This doctrine of delay, of shunning excitement upon a subject which ought always to excite men more than anything else can, and which ought to cause them to be in the greatest possible haste, is a delusion and trap of the devil, in which he has caught thousands of souls.

STRUGGLING and distressed Christian, when we meet in heaven where will be that heart-break that you told me of?

Will you not look me in the eyes and *laugh* to think you told me that your heart was breaking?

FROM my window I saw, after the last dreadful storm, a ship struggling into port. Her sides were all chafed and scarified, as if she had been beset by the robber waves and forced to battle for her life. Her mast was broken, her sails draggled and torn. Her spars and yards were gone, and she looked almost a wreck.

Out on the sea the waves had risen against her, and all the thievish winds had sought to do her harm. A desperate time she had indeed of it, but she had made her port; and now, as she dropped her anchor and lay securely in her moorings, her hull sound, her cargo all safe, her crew alive and well, what to her was it that she had been obliged to fight her way, or that out at sea the waves and winds were even yet raging and mad with storms? She had gained her harbor; she had made a prosperous voyage. The end for which she was sent forth she had accomplished —not the less nobly that through storm and tempest she had held upon her way.

But what was it to the ship John Milton, when she was floating, piece by piece, upon the waves—when her cargo was all sunken, and her crew all drowned and lying on the beach, or in the sea—that all the first part of her voyage had been pleasant, that all the middle of it had been over smooth and sunny seas, that she had passed in safety all the islands, and sailed prosperously over the equator? Her voyage was a failure, for she never entered port. The end—the *end* stamps a career as successful or disastrous; and the John Milton did not answer the end for which she was sent forth.

Men are as ships sent forth upon the sea, and that man who gains the port of heaven, though he be more battered and bruised than any ship that ever sailed up yonder river to its anchorage, he is the successful man; but he who founders on the beach, no matter how close it be to the open gates of heaven, has made a bad voyage, though his log-book may tell of sunshine and fair winds all the way to the shoal whereon he struck and found destruction.

GOD'S *glory* is his *goodness*. This, by his own showing.

THE ship of morality draws too much water ever to ride into the harbor of salvation. No one ever was or ever will be able to enter with her. Her keel always reaches too far down. A lighter craft must be obtained, or you will be forever outside of moorings.

In man's natural state, he inhabits only the ground floor of his soul's dwelling—the apartments which look out upon the back yard, where is accumulated all the filth and garbage of the household. The upper apartments are all fastened up and injured from disuse.

When a man has deliberately and understandingly resolved to turn from all his evil ways and devote himself heart and soul to the service of God, he is converted. There has been too much fog and darkness thrown about this simple matter of conversion. The whole difference in the state of a justified man and a man under condemnation is, that one uses himself first for God and his fellow creatures, and the other uses himself first for *himself*, and second only (if at all) for God and his fellows. There are multitudes of men who would like to be Christians, if they only knew how; but they are waiting to be struck by some mysterious and romantic flash, which will never come. If they feel like praising and loving now, let them do it; there is no danger of its being wrong. Many wish to be able to *begin* their Christian course with joy and triumph. Let them begin, even if it be in darkness and doubt. The joy and triumph will await them at the other end.

If I had only had somebody to tell *me* the things that I now tell *you*, how much trouble I should have escaped! I used to sing hymns from the outside, just as hungry boys, who have no pennies, look in at bake-shops, through the windows.

"Ah!" I used to think, smelling the hymns, "I, too, *could* enjoy them, just as all these Christians do; but they are not for me. *I* am not a Christian." Now, I say, if there is any one in this lecture-room, who is holding his heart back from feelings that he thinks should belong only to Christians, unhand yourselves; give your heart its will; let it rise, exult, love and praise. God is working in you. To check these feelings, or to hide them, is to smother the Holy Spirit. There is no reason why any soul before me this hour should not resolve to take Jesus Christ for his Lord and love, and rise up from his seat a converted man. There is no need to go days and weeks under conviction of sin. It is no credit to a man to have a terrible time being converted. It is a mean business. Suppose that I had lied to my partner in business. Suppose he were to charge it upon me, and I were to try to evade the matter, and were to oblige him to chase me through a whole week, crowding me here, poking me there, and pressing me in every possible way to own my fault; until at last he cornered me so closely, that seeing escape to be impossible, I gave in, and said, "Well, I *have* lied, and I am sorry;" just because I could not help yielding. How mean a spirit should I thus show. How much better, if upon sudden press of temptation I had sinned, for me to stop at once when the lie was charged upon me, and say honestly, blushing crimson with shame, "Yes, yes, I am wrong, all wrong. I am sorry, and will do so no more."

Why will not men, when they see their guilt and danger, face right about and make short work with themselves?

Mirth is the sweet wine of human life. It should be offered sparkling with zestful life unto God. He desires no emasculated or murdered offerings.

That which is wickedness *per se* in man would be infinitely worse in God.

Christians all ought to reflect the character of Christ. But the young Christian says: "It cannot be that the Spirit of God is really in me, or I should be more like brother so and so. He, now, seems a good deal like Christ, but who ever would guess what Christ was like, if he judged by me? I wish my experiences were like that good brother's." Now suppose the flowers in a garden were to say: "Since the rose is the queen of flowers, she should be our example; we should all bud, and leaf, and blossom, just as the rose does, if we wish to do it right."

But you say: "The work of the Spirit of God should be the same, should it not? *Is it* ever the same? Does God allow any two men ever to perform the same radical acts in the same manner? Does he not seem to abhor sameness? Your Christian graces must be such as consist with your original nature, the character and disposition which God implanted in you at your birth. Your experiences will be such as consist with your education and circumstances; they will be unlike those of any other person. And you must not be discouraged because they do not now shine as do the graces of the older Christian; nor think your graces are worthless because they are yet unpolished. The negro slave in Brazil, when he works the diamond mines, is allowed his freedom when he finds an unusually large diamond.

A poor slave who has never seen any diamonds but those that are worn upon the breasts of his master, his mistress, and their family and friends, is sent to the mines. Working away there, he picks up a large stone which looks as if it might be a diamond, if it was only bright; but the negro don't know what to think of it. He says it can't be a diamond; but a companion thinks that it is one. The slave takes it to his master, who seizes it with exclamations, and declares to the slave: "You are a free man. There never before was such a diamond found in these mines!"

"What! massa!" says the trembling slave, in great trepidation and bewilderment of joy; for bad as freedom is for negroes, it always excites in them powerful emotions of pleasure. "What, massa? dat dull stone a diamond? It don't look nothing like what massa wear in his shirt bosom."

"But, don't you know, Sambo, that diamonds have always to be taken to the lapidary, and ground and polished, sometimes for two or three years, before they are ready to wear? This is a most valuable diamond; and you are, from this very moment, a free man."

There are diamonds in the rough among you; but you will be ground and polished in good time. The Lapidary has you in hand.

There are men who hold themselves aloof and look askance on this mighty revival.* They see men hurrying along at noon towards the various prayer-meetings, and they say: "It's a fever which must have its way, and then it will subside." They see a young man going to the meeting, and think it nothing to excite interest. They do not know that that

* The great revival of 1857–8.

young man had come up to a point where, if nothing had occurred to save him, he would have been bound over to destruction at the very next step. They do not see, in some far distant village, the mother or the sister praying and weeping for *him*—no sound of a father's groan is heard—none of these things—the petitions that for years have assailed the heavens, both day and night, do not cling about the youth as he walks the street; but that prayer-meeting God made to answer the desire of the parents, and to bring salvation to the son. And, eternity will show that the young man's walking towards that place of prayer was the beginning of his march to heaven.

I WOULD rather be reckoned with the lowest and meanest children of God, than take rank with the crowned kings of the earth. I am sorry that all Christians don't live so as to glorify their heavenly Father; but even as they are, I would rather clasp in my embrace the most imperfect one who really *is* born of God, than to link hands with monarchs. Where is the man (there *are* creatures by courtesy *called* men who are ashamed of their old-fashioned parents, or of their country relatives when they meet them in the city streets—it would take a regiment of these miscreants to make a decent-sized hair for the head of a genuine *man*) who would not rush from the presence and communion of princes, if he saw on some forlorn and ragged little child in the street, the lineaments of his father or his mother, and knew that the wanderer was his own brother? Do you think that man would not choose the ragged child to a dozen princes? And in the Christian's face I ever see the lineaments of my beloved Father—God.

A REVIVAL is as when a sportsman goes out with his gun, and sends its charge into a flock of pigeons. Some fall dead at once, and he sees and secures them; but others, sorely hurt, limp off and hide, to die among the bushes. The best part of this* revival is, that while you can only see those who are shot dead and fall down before you, there are, thank God! thousands in all parts of the land, being hit and wounded, to go off unnoticed to their own homes, and God heals them there.

You will bear me witness that two years ago, when we were right in the midst of the great political excitement of 1856, I said once and again, that it was utterly impossible to intone the

* The great revival of 1857–8.

American public so with the sentiment that Christianity must enter into and rule in politics as truly and entirely as elsewhere, without laying the foundations for a revival of religion as broad as the whole land. The seed then sown is now ripening.

I THINK, when men sincerely try to work for God and souls, they are as men who go out to sow seed in a windy day. A few, very few may drop where they think that they sow all; and when they go to seek for fruit, lo! there is but a handful, and the men are disappointed and grieved. But their seed is growing in other fields, by the wayside, on the mountains, in the forest, everywhere; and at the end they shall be astonished to behold their harvest.

WE say to men, are you willing to serve Christ, and to love him? They answer readily—"Yes, we are; but we want to be *converted.*" By this they mean that they want to have *all that blessedness of sensation* that they have heard about; they want to find that every tendency and aptitude to sin is cut up by the roots. They want to be converted so that they'll never have anything more to do but to feel the joy of salvation. They want God to do all their fighting for them, and that is what he never will do. When a man is converted, he is *set right*, armed for conflict, and ordered to *go on* through his enemies, until he reaches heaven. He often *must* have hard and bitter times in his struggles with himself; but God's grace will be his stay and consolation, and at the other end he will find what he is too apt to look for at this.

I HAVE hope, I have courage. Our churches are certainly purifying themselves; they are coming up to a higher type of religion. That John Baptist work before our last election prepared the way, and we *are* going forward. A speech like that just made in this meeting,* twenty years ago would have blown it up like a bombshell; now I don't think that we have even lost grace or good nature through it. God used to walk by *inches; now* he goes by seven-league strides.

THIS one thing I have noticed in everybody—the moment they come to a clear apprehension of the love of Christ, they turn right about upon the minister, or upon the Christians who have been laboring, perhaps for years, to bring them to that very

* By a well-known anti-slavery man.

point, and say, "Why didn't you tell us this before?"

Why, it's what we've been *always* telling them. I think that trying to point a man to the love of Jesus is like trying to show one a star that has just come out, the only star in the whole cloudy sky.

"I can see no star," says the man. "Where is it?"

"Why, there; don't you see?"

But the man shakes his head; he can see nothing. But by and by, after long looking, he catches sight of the star; and now he can see nothing else for gazing at it. He *wonders* that he had not seen it before.

Just so it is with the soul that is gazing after the star of Bethlehem. Nothing in the world seems so hidden, so complex, so perplexing, as this thing, until it is once seen by the heart, and then, oh! there never was anything that ever was thought of that is so clear, so simple, so transcendently glorious. And men marvel that the whole world does not see and feel as they do.

I THINK that I am a man-of-war, and every gun in me is a fifty-four-pounder; and when circumstances call for the grace of indignation, I can bear my part; but wrath is not so good as love.

The everlasting God, who sitteth at the head and top of universal dominion, makes himself the servant of the very least and lowest of his creatures. Should we, then, be too proud to help each other? Should we scorn to lend our help, or influence, or sympathy, to the *least* among our brothers? How despicable must such a disposition in us look to God.

There is nothing of which men know less than of themselves. They do not understand how their own characters are formed; they stand in great doubt as to their own moral states before God. They cannot judge or take account of themselves, much less of their fellows. It is a great comfort to know that there is One who perfectly knows all that is in us, and all that concerns us; and who will take us for just our real worth. It is a comfort to trust in God. Oh! when a little child is weary, marching through a desert towards his home, when he feels that he has no longer strength to travel, nor wisdom to direct his way, how glad is he to have his father take him in his arms to rest him. And when the child, just before falling asleep, raises his eyes for one more glance at the face above him, and sees it firm and calm and set for home, how sweetly he resigns himself to slumber, confident that all is well. And thus do we, in the weary march through life, sometimes love to recline upon the bosom of the Eternal Traveller, and take our hour of rest confiding in our God.

THERE are men in this congregation who are in the situation of undermined towers of a beleaguered city. I have seen the enemy hollowing them out at the foundations, I have seen the kegs of gunpowder rolled in, and the train laid, and now I see the enemy hiding just behind his covert, with his slow match in his hand, waiting for the word to fire the train. I have warned the fated men, but they will not heed me. I cannot even pray for them any more; but I live in daily expectation of the explosion; I wait the hour which shall blow them to destruction; for I know, almost as though it were already passed, that their doom is sealed.

Now if any of you before me tremble, and think, despairingly, "It is I," probably it is not you. The anxious and troubled ones are not those who are given over to ruin.

WE are all so imperfect, that when we really consider of our case, remembering that God sees us as if by candles, into the very darkest parts of ourselves, we wonder how he can *love* even the best of us. All men believe that God exercises a *general* benevolence towards men; but that his feelings towards them amount to actual *love*—yearning, tender, desiring love, and that in regard to the most wicked, the prowling thief, the vile lecher, the lost and desperate—even the murderer. This is what staggers us. That he loves not only his elect, who strive to serve him, but wretches, just because it is in his own disposition to love what *needs* love, is our God's chief glory. That he has something in his pure and holy nature which causes him to love sinners, while he abhors their sins, is Gospel teaching. Herein lies our hope and our salvation, for it was while we were yet at enmity with God that he sent his Son to die for us.

A PIRATE cannot be pardoned for his piracy because he is generous, and in most respects a moral fellow. He is out on the high seas as a pirate, and is game for hemp and gallows, though he read his Bible every day, and do a thousand kind and good actions every week. But if he repent of his ways, and try to become an honest seaman, a few forgetful oaths may be forgiven him. If he is sailing right, and with right intentions, he will not be strictly dealt with, though he do knock down a man now and then when he ought not. So a man who has not accepted Christ as his

Saviour, who is using himself just as God did not intend that he should be used, need not hope that his occasional good and generous deeds can do him any service in the matter of salvation. A man who has given himself to Christ can be forgiven and helped anew, if he halt and stumble, because his face is set in the right way, and his heart's desire is that he may attain unto a perfect obedience. His sins will be each day pardoned by the mercy of him to whom he looks for all of this life, and that which is to come.

THERE are no troubles which have such a wasting and disastrous effect upon the mind, as those which must not be told; but which cause the mind to be continually rolling and turning over upon itself, in ceaseless convolutions and unrest.

THERE are a thousand things which between the right persons are pure, but which are so sacred and delicate that the merest touch from the world cannot be given without causing the utmost pain. One who would go eavesdropping to catch the confidences of parent and child, husband and wife, or lover and lover, and would then, to the distress and confusion of those concerned, report what he had heard, is a scoundrel.

The common way of representing God as being very anxious for and jealous of his own glory, has a bad influence on the minds of men until they justly understand what his glory is. We are not left in doubt as to that. Moses prayed and said, "I beseech thee, show me thy glory." And the Lord passed by, proclaiming, not might, majesty, and dominion, not omnipotence, nor any awful attribute, but, "The Lord, the Lord God, merciful and gracious, long suffering and abundant in goodness and truth." These are the things in which God places his glory; and this is the glory which man is called upon to promote, and which God is bent upon preserving.

The old-fashioned lightning-rods were made all in one; and when they drew the bolt it came with mighty force, and the crash often did much damage; but now the old plan is improved, and by having many points to the rod the lightning is scattered, and made to strike with greatly divided and diminished force, and to sink harmlessly to the earth. If conviction were to strike the sinner as lightning strikes the first sort of rod, the man could no more live than he could were he to look into the face of God. But through the mercy of Jesus Christ, it strikes only point by point, a separated and enfeebled force. There is no need, in most cases, that it should be otherwise. More feeling than is needed to produce right action is unnecessary. God be thanked that we are *not* allowed to see all the plague of our own hearts!

THERE is no mercy nor pardon for any man who does not feel himself utterly helpless and lost. A *hopeless* sinner is the only one who has reason *to hope* for forgiveness. If a man comes to Christ asking only a little help, thinking that he can patch himself up with that, without the humiliating confession of *utter* unworthiness, he will get nothing.

THERE are materials enough in every man's mind to create a hell there.

WHEN my head, that is worth so little, aches, I feel it to be unspeakable relief that I may lay it upon his breast whose head is worth so much. God's head never aches. He does not have to study. He sees—sees the naked soul of every creature. When the apostle says to the Jews that the word of God is quick and powerful, etc., he brings to their mind the idea of the priest's examination of the sacrificial victims. The Hebrew priests not only examined each animal externally, but they also took the beast and split him open at the back bone, and made a minute investigation into his internal state, before he was offered. This habit was the foundation of the form of expression in the verse ; * and then the apostle goes on to say, that before God *every* creature is laid open, as the sacrificial beast was before the priest. The argument which he draws in these verses seems at a first view to be a strange one; but the apostle always speaks from depths which the world knows not how to sound. God's perfect knowledge of us, of all our countless interlacing thoughts, of the checkered play of all our passions, of all our acts and motives, of the very darkest and foulest pits and crevices down to the very bottom of our souls. The idea of his escapeless gaze, why it seems *terrible*, if we think of him only from the standpoint of our sins; but when we begin to consider his perfect love, and his perfect honor, that he has known us from everlasting, even as he knows us now, and that he is never surprised (as we are ourselves) at anything we do, but has sworn to give us everlasting life, and to cleanse us from all unrighteousness, if we only trust to him, we can begin to understand that, *because* he knows us, we may come *boldly* to his footstool for help in every time of trouble. I think it is not safe or best for us to give

* Heb. iv. 12 *et seq.*

unreserved confidence to *any human* friend, *however* dear, for none are always altogether noble and unselfish, none that will not in some way, or at some time, abuse such confidence. The power of hiding ourselves from each other is most mercifully given, for men are wild beasts, and they would devour and destroy each other but for this protection. But into the ear of God we may pour out each secret—our very self, and the confidence will be kept sacred. He invites our confidence, not because he does not already know all that we can tell him, but for our own sake he bids us pour out our souls to him, and he will, in return for our confidences, give us pity and consolation; for he can be touched with a feeling for our infirmities.

We look on men, and judge them; but it is not right—we see but the outward appearance. I meet a man with a face so hard and grim, and an eye so cold, that I thank God that I do not live with that man. But if I could see the path by which he has come up to where he now is—if I could see how he leaned with all the weight of a once generous and confiding heart, on what failed him in time of need—if I could see how he has been stood from under, and been pierced and bored, and the very life-blood of his affections pressed out by a thousand troubles and crosses, and perhaps by *the infernal machinery of the household*, I should feel more like throwing my arms about him, and trying to console him for all that had made him what he is.

Whatever there *is* in election and reprobation—and I don't know *what* there is in them, therefore I never preach them, for I will not preach what I cannot at all understand—there certainly is nothing that hinders any man from gaining salvation. When *I* undertake to preach election, I turn to the last chapter of the Bible, and read: "And the Spirit and the Bride say come," etc. It is *the last utterance* of the sacred volume, and it is sincere. If I doubted God's perfect sincerity and simplicity, in such invitations, I should say that those who worshipped him were the sinners, and those who refused to pay him homage were the saints. I think the doctrines of the Bible are like flowers that are in the morning all covered with spiders' webs. They are obscured and mystified by miscreant theological spiders. There is nothing so simple that these men will not change it into a mystery, which they themselves, nor any who hear or study them, shall be able to understand.

A MAN who impoverishes his soul for the sake of worldly gain, is like one who, desiring to learn to play upon a harp, tears out all its strings, wherewith to pay for his tuition. He gains gold, perhaps, but when it is his, he has left to him no capacity to enjoy it.

Perfection has usually been understood to mean absence of evil, but it does not mean that any more than absence of weeds means harvest.

The Bible measure of perfection is the measure of the fullness of the stature of Jesus Christ. This ought long ago to have settled the much vexed question of Christian perfection. Until a man can measure himself by Christ, and come up to his stature, he must not claim to be perfect, and he will not arrive at that fullness in this world. Conversion is not instant deliverance from all wrong tendencies, from all errors and follies, nor even from all sins. It is but the *beginning* of a good character.

There may be instances where men are converted into a very high state of righteousness at the outset; but I *know* that this is rarely the case. Generally, the young convert is but set about, and has his way to cut through ten thousand native heart-born foes. There are his passions and his appetites that for many years have had their own headlong will; and there are all the selfish instincts; there is rampant pride to be subjugated, and the work is long and hard. But every man is encouraged to work hopefully by the command: "Work out your own salvation with fear and trembling; for it is God that worketh in you, both to will and to do of his own good pleasure." Let no hard, fault-finding man of the world look upon the Christian when he fails or falls, and say, "He is no Christian else he would do better than that." He will often fall and fail; but he must always rise again, and with renewed courage and faith go forward working out his own salvation. He *never* need despair, for *God* worketh in him, and that is strength enough for anything.

There are some men who have not much native strength or stability of character, and though while they are out of the way of trial they walk well, when they are among the every-day influences of life, they are drawn far from what they know to be right. Here in church, where there is prayer and singing, they feel all right, and are sure that they are very near to heaven; they are inspired by the spirit of the place, and feel melted with love and devotion. But to-morrow they go over to New York. They don't hear many hymns there. Religion is not much the subject of conversation and consideration over there; it is all sharpness, shrewdness, warding off, grasping stocks, money-market, etc.; and the man goes with the hurrying, hasty tide. Selfishness, duplicity, greed, are about him and within him, and so he wanders from the way and does a hundred wrong things. But by and by is his meeting evening; and among his church brethren the wavering man sits down to hear of Jesus and of duty, and of the experiences of others. The same nature that caused him to go so wrong when among those whose influence was wrong, now draws him another way. A brother rises and gives utterance to some touching thought, the man is broken down at once; tears stream down his cheeks, his heart swells, he must rise and speak—he sings with his brethren, and his face shines with inward happiness. He feels very good again; and, for the time, he is as sincere as anything can be; but the world looks on and cries, "Look at him! he is an old knave and hypocrite." He is no more a hypocrite than a thermometer is. It *may indeed be* that he is not a Christian. He whose feet are upon the Rock of Ages should stand more firmly than this; but he is sincere.

There are many Christians who in their affections are thoroughly submissive. When they suffer *there* they grow more sweet and humble—their trials make them better. Though their affections are deep and tender they bow before God when he touches their hearts in them, and they say and *feel* that he does all things well, and that he is blessed; but you take these same men and trouble them in their business, and where is their Christian submission then?—apparently they are no better than infidels. They have not educated themselves to yield their wills to the will of God in their *business* affairs; afflictions there cause them, as it seems, to grow worse and worse all the time.

At first it is sufficient that the Christian believes the truths of the Gospel because they are in the Bible, given by the Spirit of God.

When first the traveller follows the direction of the guide-board, he does so because it says that is the way to go; but when he has gone that way once, and again, and finds that it always ends just where he intended to stop, he looks at the guide-board no more. He has forgotten it, for he does not need it now. He believes in the road, because he knows by experience that it will lead him whither he desires to go.

Thus should the Christian, of ten or a score of years, believe in the vital truths of religion, not alone because Christ declares them, but because he has felt and known them in his own heart and life. Faith is first, but afterwards is actual knowledge—we do "*know* of the doctrine."

MANY persons have read the Bible so much that to them it has come to have very little practical force or meaning. A man will read aloud the passage on "charity," or "love," as it should be rendered, and not an echo of its meaning will be in his heart. He will read it reverently, as he thinks a Christian man should, and will then arise and begin straightway to be NOT "long suffering" nor "kind;" not to bear all things, believe all things, or hope all things; not to think no evil; but to *be* "easily provoked," and to behave unseemly, without one passing thought that what he has just read should have aught to do with his daily life among his associates. This scripture is thus a dead letter.

IF you desire a new church which will accommodate six thousand people, if you will raise the full amount required for its erection and furnishing, I will engage to speak in it so that all shall hear me. I will do my part in the contribution also; but I tell you beforehand, that I will have nothing to do with building a church, or with preaching in it, of which, when it is finished, even the poorest workman can truly say, as he stands and looks upon it, "I lost by that job."

If you will have such a building for me to preach in, no man, from the largest contractor down to the poorest laborer that carries a hod, must be able to say that he lost a single penny by the enterprise. Money sufficient to pay to each man what is just and right must be raised, or the matter must be dropped quicker than it was taken up. As to my being able to speak so as to be heard in any part of such a building as you contemplate, I should think you might be satisfied of *that* by the way in which I am speaking *now*.

MEN are agreed in this, that all do glory in something. Each one glories according to his society. The honesty and gentleness, the truth and guilelessheartedness, which are the glory of the true gentleman, would render a man the mark for scorn and contempt among burglars, and gamblers, and aldermen, and other thieves.

WE are not to try to crush out any quality. If we put a ball through the head of a wild young horse, he will be made quiet and harmless enough; but he will be good for nothing. The right way is to break him, and harness him; then he will be fit for use. Just so it is with the faculties of a man's mind. They all need breaking, harnessing, and right directing; but they must not be killed or maimed. That faculty whose perversion becomes pride is the gift of God, and he has given directions for its proper action. "Let him that glorieth glory in *this*, that he understandeth and knoweth me." To "glory" means to value one's self; to feel self-complacency, because of some real or fancied superiority. But we are forbidden to glory in *anything* except in our knowledge of God.

How far do men come from obedience to this injunction! They glory in everything *but* that. One walks the streets with such an air that you would say he supposes that God had fashioned a very masterpiece when he fashioned him—yet no; it is not even his body that he so much glories in, as in the things which he has stuck on to it. He glories in his dress, and in his perfumes. Another glories in his muscular form, in his fine proportions, and in his strength. He goes through the streets almost wishing that some one would come at him that he might display his power of self-defence. The pride of these men lies in the things which they possess in common with the beasts of the field. But others glory in their riches and their skill; others again in their genius. These things are not to be despised. Even riches God reckons as good; for they are among the rewards promised to those who diligently serve him. Beauty and attractiveness of person, and the possession of winning manners have this much in them: they are the gift of God; they give pleasure to others, and ought to do so to their owners. They should be a cause of gratitude, but never of "glorying." It is a sort of organic affectation with some to pretend to despise personal symmetry and beauty.

Wealth, in the economy of Providence is made a powerful means of civilization, and it is right to value it, in its place. It is good, sometimes it is even grand, to know how to fill the day with profitable transactions, to make every movement tell for the advancement of some one enterprise; but men should not glory in their business or executive force of skill, or in their sharp foresightedness. They should glory in *this* that they *understand* and know the Lord.

Perhaps there may be men now before me who are saying: "I have valued myself all wrong—God help me—I will try to benefit by this discourse;" and perhaps some man will go home and make a note in his journal to the effect that his heart was touched, and he resolved to do differently for the future. Monday morning he will rise, and as he starts for the city he will say to himself: "Now, *remember*." As he walks towards the ferry, a quick step sounds behind him, and a laughing voice says, as he gets a friendly slap on the shoulder: "Ah! ah! but that was a capital hit of yours

—that mortgage, you know—I've heard all about it. But didn't you trip that fellow's heels up well? I declare; it *was* capital."

"No! you didn't hear about it, though, did you!"

The man is instantly as full of vain glory as champagne is full of bubbles. Sunday and its impressions are forgotten; the week is here; his good resolves are gone—where the bubbles go. That one compliment in regard to an act of wicked shrewdness, has shot him all through of infernal electricity, and he is *a business man* until the next Sunday. In what does that man glory?

As we ascend in the ranks of humanity, we wonder on what the great thinkers, the great inventors, the painters, the poets, the orators, and architects, most valued themselves. We think we should like to know what Shakspeare, that great student of human nature, thought of "the immortal Will," when he, in turn, arose before him, as probably he did—and we think it would be grand to know what Dante and old Homer valued most in themselves. Then our thoughts, still lifting themselves, look on the angels, and wonder what is their self-estimate. We tremble as we approach God, and hardly dare to wish to hear in what he glories. He, infinitely above all things that are created, the architect of all architects. Why, St. Peter's is a mere rat-hole compared to the smallest worlds that God flings from his fingers faster than sparks fly from the blacksmith's anvil; but he has told us in what he glories: and first and chiefest is his "loving kindness." Not merely kindness—it is a compound word. There are ten thousand kindnesses that have in them not one spark of love; but that word, "loving," has a personal meaning—it shows us that there is the tie of affection between us and our Creator. God glories in his "loving kindness, his judgment, and his righteousness," and man should glory in understanding and trying to imitate the same.

I think it would be a good sermon for a man to take pen and paper and write down, first, all the things in which he does glory; next, the things in which he ought to glory; and then an indiscriminate list of his acts, and thoughts, and plans, and wishes. But I think it would be easier to induce men to go alone, at midnight, and in the dark, into the charnel-house, and drive a nail into a coffin, after the manner of the superstition of some, than to go down into the depths of their own selves, and write out truly, with real judgment writing, what there they would see.

Coin that is current in one place, is valueless in another. Suppose an Indian, far in the western wilds, were to say, "I will become a trader with the whites. I will go to New York city and buy up half the goods there, and come back and sell them, and then what a rich Indian I shall be." He then collects all his wampum beads, which are his money; and compared with other Indians he is very rich, and away he journeys to yonder city. Imagine him going into Stewart's, and offering his wampum there, in exchange for their goods. They are refused. They were money in the woods—in the city they are worthless. And there are thousands of men who are carrying with them, to offer at the judgment, what is no better than the Indian's beads. They are reckoning on their generosity, their prompt payment of all their debts, their various good natural qualities; but when they present them, they will all be found worthless trash. The things that have made them strong, and valued, and important here, will there be worse than useless to them.

CRITICS say that Raphael's transfiguration transgresses the rules of art. It is two pictures in one. Christ is represented upon the mountain top, in his glory, the disciples having fallen, in wonder and awe, to the earth; beneath this scene is the one of the possessed child, about whom the horror-stricken disciples stand, unable to afford relief. With the merit or fault of this double representation I have nothing to do; all that I know is this, that picture is a figure of human life. Above, Christ often hovers in glorious light; while below, the devil is tearing the child.

WHAT a man is, is not what he is on Sunday, when the organist plays to him, and the minister plays to him, and all good influences play to him; but it is what he is in the week-day, when his life is wearing, and working, and weaving for him the garment in which he is to stand and be judged.

MANY that are last shall be first, and the first shall be last. There are men whose entrance into Wall street is like the appearance of blue sky after a northeast storm. They move along, leaving a trail of bows and smiles, and heartburnings and envy behind them. How the sallow faces light up as old Moneybags approaches. He is pointed after. "Do you know him? A wonderful man!—worth his millions—smart as lightning," etc. That old obese abomination of money is their god; and yet there is not one particle of genuine worth in him. He has utterly defiled and destroyed his manhood in the manufacturing of wealth; he is a great epitomized, circulating hell on earth, and when he dies, hell will groan—one more woe.

But there are other men—they are seen sometimes; business-men say of them: "Oh, yes, we know them—clever fellows enough—mean very well—do some good among the poor—have classes in mission schools, etc. They are just suited for that; but, bless your life! there might be a million such men in the world, and nothing would ever be done."

These men die, and heaven rings with new shouts of melody. There they are known and waited for, and with triumphant joy are welcomed home.

THE artist, when he begins to learn to draw, finds the greatest difficulty in making straight lines and circles, but when he has coaxed the juice of his brain down into his fingers, so that *they* think, he has but to give one glance at the object he desires to represent, and the lines appear, the circles fly off from his fingers, and the picture is drawn, almost without thought. Thus involuntary should be right-doing with the Christian. He should form for himself a settled habit, a sort of refined, spiritual instinct, by which he should be led constantly and almost unconsciously, to shun the evil, and to choose the good.

CHRISTIAN men, what testimony does your life yield to your sons? Is it that religion, your duty to God, has the first place in your regard, and business success the subordinate place? Or is your practical life (I do not say your theoretic life, *that* is more frequently right), such as to cause them to conclude that you think religion a good thing, but that a man *must* succeed in business, anyhow, and after that he ought to serve God as well as he can.

SOME men have pronounced the rebukes of conscience to be the punishment for sin. I marvel how they can reason thus; or I should marvel if I did so at anything in man. Either all is marvellous in him, or nothing is.

But can any reasonable being believe that the Creator would institute a punishment which should deal most severely with the smallest sins, and least severely with the greatest? Would God decreee that the worst man should bear least punishment, and the best man most? Yet look at facts, and deny not that this is the way in which conscience punishes. Everybody knows that it is the first and least sins that are most soundly scourged by this feeling. It is in proportion as a man is pure that his sins afflict him. It is at the *beginning* of a wrong course that we run against the spears, that we kick against the pricks, that we are excoriated. When a man is in the deeper places of guilt, he is generally far more comfortable than he was before he had descended so low. How can any one imagine that the Almighty would contrive such a miserable, one-sided mode of punishment?

Repentance is not feeling bad about your sins, or talking humbly about them, or calling yourself hard names, or thinking that you are the greatest of sinners, or writing in your journal about your depravity, or praying, or going forward to the anxious seat; it is *turning from your sins to righteousness.* When you feel bad enough to do that, it is sufficient. More feeling is useless, and often dangerous. It is this firing up of feeling which causes most of the mischief complained of in revivals. There is no merit in deep feeling. It is no credit to a man that God was obliged to shake him over fire and brimstone to make him a convert. Turn—blessed are they who, the moment they are made to see that they are sinners, and are lost without the Saviour, go straight to him, without waiting to be lashed thither—such are the best conversions—such are the most noble natures. But some have presented God and his law in such a way, as to offend against all of taste, generosity, and manliness—I had almost said against every affection there is in man; and then they call the stirring that there is within against this view of God the rebellion of the natural heart, and they teach that there must now be a pitched battle between God and the soul—God saying, "You shall submit," and the soul declaring, "I won't;" until, finally, when driven to the very verge of perdition, by the thunders of the law, the soul turns short about and hastens to God—rather than fall into hell. There may be, there are, experiences like this, but they are not the rule, they are not needful—at least not to many. In my office of pastor, I am often called upon to talk with persons who are in trouble, because they think they were converted too easy, or because they never had such times as Payson had, when he had dyspepsia, and fasted, and had horrible views of "the exceeding sinfulness of sin." "If I was really converted, why was I not converted just as Brother A. was? If conversion is the work of God, it will be alike, won't it? There will be no mistaking it."

Men are the work of God—did ever you see *two men* who were in all respects *exactly alike*? God's taste evidently does not choose uniformity.

Two ships come into New York harbor. One has crossed the ocean with a favoring breeze. She had all sails set, everything below and aloft spread to the pleasant wind, and not one hindrance was in her way. But another soon enters, and everybody hastens to board her. The captain of the fortunate craft is one of the first to greet his brother captain: "How came you in such a plight? Did you have a storm?" he says. "Storm!" repeats the other, "I guess we did. I've been upon the ocean forty years (you know with captains the last storm is the worst that they ever saw), and I never saw a time like the one we've just passed—we've been near foundering a dozen times. We've lost our top-masts and our bowsprit, our sails are torn into ribbons, our bulwarks are stove in, we've lost our boats; I've lost all I had, and my men are nearly worn out. It has been hurricanes one side or another all the way across, and we have but just got into port alive." The captain of the uninjured ship goes back to her decks and says, dubiously, shaking his head: "Well, boys, I begin to doubt whether we really are in New York, after all. It can't be that we have crossed the ocean, *we* never had any experience *like that*."

NEVER did a summer pass that did not smite on the storehouse of autumn, and cause it to open its doors and bring forth of its abundant treasures.

There was a time when honesty, truth and fairness of general behavior were the chief things that religious teachers insisted upon; and men almost forgot that Christianity had any inner life; but the reaction came, and to this external religion arose an opposition. The defrauded faculties asserted their claim, and now was the era of intense spiritual devotees, who taught that there might be a true and vital Christianity in a man's heart, distinct from, and independent of, his outward life and conduct. It was faith and works at war with each other, and religiously bombarding each other with texts; instead of walking hand in hand in holy union. There is no way in which a man can prove that he has true faith in his heart, except by good works in his life

---

Many persons suppose that there is required, in order to a man's satisfactory conviction that he is a child of God, a vivid and unmistakable assurance of faith. They think that the heart is as wax, and like inert wax they suppose it lies, until the Lord takes his signet ring or seal, and stamps it with his name. Then, after feeling that impression, the soul is certain of its son-ship. It may wander away, and the name may be covered from sight by ten thousand faults and sins, but down beneath them all, it is *there*, and it cannot be erased. Now this is not the way in which the Spirit of God usually bears witness with our spirit that we are the sons of God. Without doubt there is immediate actual contact of God's Spirit with the spirit of man, whenever this is best; but ordinarily all our experiences are made to come to us through the medium of our own natural states; through the influences of things around us, and within us. *Anything* that produces in the mind the reasonable, sober conviction that we are his, is the true witness of God's Spirit with ours. The evidences of a man's Christianity (if he *is* a Christian) are not so difficult and serious a matter as men think. Why, any one who has sense sufficient to judge whether he is a good citizen or not, or whether he is the affectionate son of his own parents, can tell whether he is a child of God. "If ye love me ye will keep my commandments." "Ah!" you sigh, "but I don't always keep them." Well, ask that little child how he knows that he loves his parents; he will answer you, "Because I love to do what they want me to do." "Why, my dear child, you are always doing what they *don't* want you to do. You can't prove your love to them by that rule." The poor child hangs its head, and says, "I don't know as I can." He cannot answer you. You ask again, "My child, how do you *know* that you love your parents?" "Why, why I *do* love to please them better than anything else in the world." "Ah! but I have just shown you that you do not always try to please them; how can you say that *this* is your proof of love to them?" The child is silenced; but in his little heart he knows that in spite of his disobedience he does desire to do his parents' will; and that he *does* love them, whether he perfectly obeys them or not. He thinks, perhaps, "I am a poor child, a hard child to manage; I give them a great deal of trouble, but I love them; I am their own child after all. They would never give me up; and nothing on earth could take me from them."

Faith is the life of a child, and that is why the Saviour declares, "Except ye become as little children, ye shall not enter the kingdom of heaven." When, therefore, you examine yourself by the rule of obedience, and find that you are not perfect there, see if it is your greatest desire to honor Christ by keeping his commandments, and if you are trying to do so; and if it is the grief and pain of your life that you fail as you do. If you wish, more than anything else, to be his; if you yearn to have him for your friend; if you feel that *you must and will belong to him or to nobody*, you need no more remarkable "witness." If you were not his before, you are so now; so enjoy him afresh—*'tis sweet making love again.*

Suppose one of the sheep in a fold were to go to the shepherd, and say, "I think I'm your sheep, because you get six pounds of wool off me;" and another should say, "And I think I'm your sheep, because you get four pounds of wool from me;" and a third, "I hope I am your sheep, but I don't know, for you only get three pounds of wool from me; and sometimes it is but two." Finally, suppose one poor scraggy fellow comes who don't know whether he is a sheep or a goat, and makes his complaint; the shepherd would say, "I know who are the best sheep, and who are the worst. I wish you could all give me ten pounds of wool; but whether you give me ten pounds or one, you are all mine. I bought you, and paid for you, and you are all in my fold, and you every one belong to me." It is not how much a sheep brings his owner which proves him his. The proof that the sheep belongs to the shepherd is, that the shepherd bought him and takes care of him.

The main thing is to be determined to go towards heaven. If the man resolutely aims for that place, he will not fail to reach it in the end, however much he may wander off his track; pushed this way and that by temptations. The most unskillful navigator may gain the port for which he steers, even though his course across the sea be zigzag, if every time he takes the sun he comes back to his course, and perseveres in his endeavors to gain his desired haven. He may justly say: "Though I am a bungler, and a very poor navigator, I am no smuggler, no pirate; I work hard to gain my port, and I believe that I shall gain it in safety." Thus the Christian often is constrained to cry out: "Lord, thou knowest that I mean to hold an even course towards thee; but thou knowest, also, how I am pushed off here by wrong impulses, and drawn off there by vain desires—how pride, and vanity, and selfishness impede my way; and how often my appetites and passions trip up my feet, and cast me to the earth. Yet I will come back to the path. I do desire to keep it. The settled and deliberate resolve and aspiration of my soul is to walk in the way of thy commandments."

When I was at Fall River, I was obliged to rise at four o'clock in the morning to take the train. I took my carpet-bag in my hand and ran, but was in trouble lest I might be running directly from the cars instead of towards them. There was not a person in sight; but I saw a light in one upper window. A watcher was there. I rang the bell, and asked information as to my way. It was given.

I was about right—only needed a little help; and now, knowing that I was in the right way, I did run. A bird might have counted it doing well to keep up with me; for I expected every moment to hear the bell, and the rushing off of the train, and then I should be there and my people without a sermon for Sunday. Only let me be sure that I was in the right way, and I was willing to run. So says the Christian: "*Only* let me be *sure* that I am on my way to heaven, and there is nothing that I am not willing to do or to bear."

Well, if you are so earnest, know that Christ is the way; and if you *are* desirous to cast away all that shall hinder your race, I think you need not doubt that you are already in it.

THERE is nothing on earth better than a good woman; and there is nothing on earth worse than a wicked one. The nature of a true, pure-hearted woman is lifted up until it well-nigh touches that of angels; but the nature of a bad woman strikes beneath, until her roots are fed by the fiery sap of hell.

THERE are some things that money cannot buy. The spot of land where your child lies buried, could it buy *that?* Or the last letter or gift of the best friend that you ever had on earth?

Ahab was just such a man as would have done to appoint governors for Kansas. He could cause the doing of mean and wicked acts, and yet not know anything about them. He was not responsible for the murder of Naboth—of *course* not—how should he know what his wife intended? He knew that she had promised him the vineyard; and he knew that when *she* had determined to give it to him, it was already as good as his. He was aware, also, that the woman who was thus pledged to oblige him knew no law which could stand a moment against her desires. Resolute, crafty, cruel, *not* "hard faced;" for she was, probably, very beautiful, she marched straight on to the accomplishment of her purposes, whatever might be trampled under her feet in her way. But he gave no orders; he merely said: "There is my desk, Jezebel; there is my pen, my papers, and my signet; use them as you choose. Of course, you will do nothing wrong." Imagine the two to look at each other just here. "Of *course*, Jezebel, you will do nothing wrong."

No doubt Naboth might have had twice the worth of his vineyard had he chosen to sell it. He might have had a great deal better land, and have raised three times as many grapes. But he knew that there were some crops raised on his farm which he could get nowhere else. The larger yield of grapes might be very well in their way; but he, beneath the trees and the vines under which his fathers had for generations sat, and where, beside his mother, he had sported when a child, and where his brothers and sisters were born, could drink sweeter nectar out of airy cups, than all the juice of grapes ever pressed upon the hills of Samaria. Naboth was right to hold on to his home. There were garnered memories that all the wealth of Ahab could not buy.

But Jezebel wrote her letters to the elders and to the nobles of her kingdom—to the "*Elders* and the *Nobles!*"—and she ordered them to proclaim a *fast.* When people meditate a deed of wickedness particularly atrocious, they *often* feel that they had better have a fast first. What devout men those "Elders" must have been! and how noble those "Nobles!" How acceptable to God must such fasts be! And they set Naboth on high among the people, and the false witnesses were found; no trouble about that, when the queen commanded it, and the good man was dragged out and stoned, and dogs licked his blood. Well! Naboth deserved his fate—he was "an agitator." He agitated the king; he would not let him have his vineyard for a kitchen garden; and Ahab was so agitated about it that he couldn't eat his dinner; and that agitated Jezebel very much. She did not like to see the king rolled over on the bed, like a great baby, with his face to the wall. And *they* were "the government"—so Naboth *was* an agitator of the government of his country; and he deserved stoning.

When this agitator was dead, Ahab went down to take possession of the coveted vineyard, which, as its owner had died as a criminal, lapsed from his heirs to the crown.

As the king was complacently viewing his prize, lo! there stood before him, the first growth of this desired garden, sprung to full size in one night—the prophet who was sent to pronounce to the wicked monarch his doom.

"In the place where the dogs licked the blood of Naboth shall dogs lick thy blood—even *thine*—and the dogs shall eat Jezebel by the walls of Jezreel." And this was literally fulfilled; for they were soon after miserably slain and dog eaten. When Ahab and Jezebel laid their plans, and executed their wickedness, they had forgotten God. Men do so still. Because he that sitteth in the heavens keeps quiet, they think that he is not regarding; but he is. Poor Naboth may have felt that the Lord knew not his wrongs and his distress, but we see how that was. And we see, too, by this account, how God looks upon the unrighteous actions caused by the hands of agents. Ahab was not going to hold himself accountable for the results of what Jezebel, his agent, chose to do. God, however, held him to a strict account. Retribution has a long arm; it reaches down through many years, and it is a sheriff from which there is no escape, however skillfully we may dodge all others. Thousands and ten thousands of men, would they speak out their secret convictions, would say that the very wickedness upon which they had built their highest hopes of worldly prosperity and happiness was the opening of the pit which whelmed them in destruction.

We must not too sharply blame the elders and the nobles for their part in this matter. They were but obeying the law. They did not want to trouble their minds, or endanger their interests, about the wild and romantic notions of "the higher law." As good citizens they must obey the requirements of government.

This is exactly what was done in our country at the time of the enactment of the fugitive slave law, and there were not wanting efforts to induce the clergy to exhort the people to submit to the law's requirements, and to aid in its enforcement.

The young ministers were very refractory; but there were numbers of the old, and hitherto respected and honorable clergymen, who were prevailed upon to aid in trying to cloak that enormous iniquity. They did *not* cloak it; they only uncloaked themselves.

Daniel Webster stooped to influence these men to this step, both by letters and by personal address, and it was taken. When our own elders advocate the enforcement of this manner of government, why should we bear too severely upon the elders who procured the death of Naboth?

It is not worth while for any one who is yet young, who has not yet soiled virtue, or honesty, or manly honor, to try the effect of doing so. Young men, be true to virtue, be honest, be religious, so shall you have peace in your later years.

A Christian, just born into the kingdom, is often like a loaf of bread when its materials are just put together. The baker has mixed them, and left the bread to rise. You go to the dough and say, "Are *you* bread?" "No," says the dough, "I am not." In an hour you go again and ask, "*Are* you bread?" "No, I am not," replies the dough; "I feel a little stirring" (said with a rising of the shoulders) "in me, but I am not bread." In two hours more you try, "Are you bread now?" "No," is still the reply, "I'm sponge; but not bread. I'm not baked, nor eaten yet." But by and by, after the baker gives it the final kneading, and it is ready for the oven, when it is *baked*, it owns that now it is really bread. Yet it has gained no new element since the first mixing. The kingdom of heaven in the heart is like leaven which a woman hid in a measure of meal until the whole was leavened.

It has been said that a statesman will not soil his hands by doing the vile and dirty work that is demanded by the present system of politics; but that he keeps for his use persons who are not squeamish as to what they do, so long as they are well paid for it. But the story of Ahab tells how that sort of management is dealt with by the Lord.

There are men in these cities known as abolitionists who, when occasion calls for it, shut their eyes and bid their southern agent do the best he can for them. They say, "I must do business; and I can't afford to lose ten thousand dollars by my southern customers. 'Tis a bad affair, no doubt. Don't let me hear a word about it. Here, I leave the matter with you. Do the best you can for me. I *wash my hands of the whole business.*"

Ah! it's rather difficult getting that sort of stain off. I tell you, the pious merchant, seated in his slippers comfortably by his Sunday fire, reading his religious paper, while his agent at the South is selling men, women, and children, body and soul too often, is held accountable for all the wrong, disaster and misery thus caused.

Don't you believe it? I appeal to God's judgment bar; and we will take up the subject and debate it again there.

Any dishonest deed done by the most extensive and respected firm—the making out of false bills of sale—the giving in of wrong invoices at the custom-house—no matter if these things be done by the hand of the greenest clerk or the last and smallest boy employed in the business, will be reckoned for, *first* and *most rigorously*, with the first in power in that firm.

Ah! there is a great deal of craft and cunning among men—they are very shrewd and subtile, and can go far and long in artifice and duplicity; but *God* is a match for them all.

A GREEDY man is not long in growing covetous, and when the grasping and avaricious passions become swollen and inflamed, there is always danger that they will break out into some deeds of deeper wickedness. He who finds himself feeling sorry that another's house is larger and better, or that his prospects in life are fairer than his own, may be sure that the worst form of envy is upon him; before he knows it, he will covet that which is another's; and then he will be in perpetual danger of committing crime, in order to obtain it. The more he looks at what he wants, the more he will want it; which is always the case with us when we want what we must not have. It is right to wish to have good things like those owned by our neighbors, if we can make fair trade for them; and if our neighbor is willing to sell that which is his, we have a right to wish for and purchase that; but our desire must go no further than this. The moment we *cherish* a desire to get from him that with which he does not wish to part, we sin. The desire, cherished, to steal makes a man a thief.

When an old man, who has spent seventy long years in this world, who has seen almost the whole of life, and is trembling on the very verge of the grave, comes at last to the Saviour, drawn by that gracious Spirit that will save unto the uttermost rather than permit the prayers of his saints to be in vain, I am glad that his soul is saved—glad for his sake—glad for the sake of the parents long ago gone home, and glad for the sake of the other faithful friends who have prayed scores and scores of years for his conversion; but after all, 'tis *a mean business.*

This giving all the greenness and efflorescence of

one's life—all one's strength and beauty—to the devil, and then, when one has sucked all the pleasures that he can get out of sin and the world, coming and offering the dregs of his life—his old worn-out corn-husk, to the Lord! 'tis *dirt mean!* If any of you young people meditate such a course, you will not be likely to be allowed the chance.

I AM not afraid of a laugh, even in the meeting-house, nor on the Sunday, if it come of a right spirit. It is often better to laugh than to weep; and to laugh in the very presence of our Maker is well, if it be the laughter of Abraham, and not the scornful and unbelieving laughter of Sarah.

WHY is it, when the coffin is unearthed, and that which has lain long within it is exposed, and when the father and the mother, bending over it with tears and anguish, call tenderly with the soul's utmost yearning: "My son! my son!" that the dust makes no reply? Why is not the mouldering mass moved? Why does it make no sign, but only the nimble worms creep in and out, and the noisome dust settles closer together? It is because the man is *dead.*

Why is it, when lover calls to lover to return,

when the confiding one who has believed in man, as she should believe alone in her God, and has been *rewarded*—as *man* rewards—pleads with the miscreant who has stolen from her her store of love, making no requital, when her tear-dimmed eyes and quivering lips beseech him, when all her soul is poured before him, and she utters her hopeless cry in his very ear, does he not pity and regard her? It is because the wretch is dead, *dead.* Dead to all that lifts him above the brute; dead to whatever is not earthly, sensual, devilish. And God calls to men, he wooes them, he entreats them, and they answer not, nor hear, because, as he declares, "They are *dead* in trespasses and sins."

The man who designedly wins the love of a woman when he knows that he either cannot or ought not fully to requite it—there is not an evil thing on the earth or beneath it that is so base a knave as he.

When you come to Christ you *must* come as an offender—you must be sorry for your sins, and perfectly willing to give them all up, or he will never receive you. Suppose a man were to strike a child, or a sick man, or a feeble woman, everybody would cry "shame!" But if he, upon reflection, grew ashamed, and went humbly and confessed his fault, and tried all in his power to make up for it, men would let him up. If, however, the man who struck happened to be one of your *consistent* men, obstinate and conceited (whose consistency is not in never *doing* wrong, but in never *confessing* it), he won't repent, nor atone. He will say, "Well, I *did* it, and it must *remain*." The world will call that man a brute. In these things the judgment of the world is that of Christ.

Suppose a man were to call upon the physician and say, "Well, sir, I want your services."

"Are you sick?" says the physician.

"No; not that I know of."

"What, then, do you want of me?"

"Oh! I want your services."

"But what for?"

The man makes no reply.

"Are you in pain?"

"No."

"Is your head out of order?"

"No."

"Nor your stomach?"

"No; I believe not. I feel perfectly well; but still I thought I should like a little of your help."

What would a doctor think of such a case as this? What must Christ think of those that ask his help, not feeling that they really *need* it?

THE Jews were as pious as people are now-a-days. They hated everybody that didn't belong to their church. They looked upon the Canaanites just as *we* look on infidels, heathens, and *abolitionists.*

I THINK that one reason for my great love for trees, and flowers, and birds is, that through the gentle ministrations of these things I was taught a better way of prayer than any which before I had known. I found my way to God stepping on the soft green leaves, and lifted by the songs of birds.

WHEN men complain to me of low spirits, I tell them to take care of their health, to trust in the Lord, and to *do good*, as a cure.

MAN'S face is a disturbed face; it shows that in his soul there is no rest, not even in his home. Disquiet is with him in the broodings of the night, and repose comes not with the flush of morning.

ATTEMPT to be aristocratic in the church, and the church dies. Its true power consists in cutting the loaf of society from top to bottom.

TIME is to us as a beleaguering army; parallel after parallel is drawn around us, and ever and anon we see an enemy's flag waving over some outwork. Charge after charge is made against us; and as sight, and hearing, and touch, fail before the assaulting army, O woe to man if he has no hereafter as a final citadel into which to retreat.

ASK any man and he will tell you, "I expect to live again." All men believe it; but this cold faith of the head is a different thing from that certainty which sometimes thrills through the heart, and makes us long for the future life, as a schoolboy longs for his father's house.

THERE is a pass beyond which no man's honor can go. Beware the narrow and intense moment of the pressure of temptation.

IT is time we were done talking of death as "The Great Tyrant," "The Enemy," etc. Death—it is only God's call, "Come home." It is but the messenger to bring them home sent to homesick children at a boarding-school; or the permission to return to his native land sent to an exile.

RELIGION is the Bread of Life. I wish we better appreciated the force of this expression. I remember what bread was to me when I was a boy. I could not wait till I was dressed in the morning, but ran and cut a slice from the loaf—all the way round, too, to keep me until breakfast; and at breakfast, if diligence in eating earned wages, I should have been well paid. And then I could not wait for dinner, but ate again, and then at dinner; and I had to eat again before tea, and at tea, and lucky if I didn't eat again after that. It was bread, bread, all the time with me, bread that I lived on and got strength from. Just so religion is the bread of life; but you make it cake—you put it away in your cupboard and never use it but when you have company. You cut it into small pieces and put it on china plates, and pass it daintily round instead of treating it as bread; common, hearty bread, to be used every hour.

A MAN'S *ledger* does not tell what he is worth. Count what is *in* a man, not what is *on* him, if you would know whether he is rich or poor.

LOVE that has no fear of God is always false and weak.

Of all impotent creatures, man is weakest, when he attempts by his own strength to put himself down. It is ocean trying to put down waves with waves. No storms are like the storms that rise when man attempts to conquer his passions.

There are days when the blood flows like wine—days when the sky is blue, and the birds sing and the flowers blossom, and are sweet about us—when life is an anthem and a delight, and on such days this world's joy and love suffice us. But a change comes soon, and when we are weary and disappointed, when the skies lower into sombre night, when there is no song of birds, and the perfume of the flowers is but their dying breath, when all is dreary autumn; *then* we yearn for him who sits with the eternal summer of love in his soul; and we know that all earthly affection is but a glow-worm's light, compared to that which blazes with such effulgence in the heart of God.

When a man gives proof that his heart is sound, and that his life is sound, there is no divergence of opinion that should keep us from fellowship with him. I am sensitive in behalf of theologies; but when theology puts its hoot upon the living, palpitating heart, my heart cries out against it

Those truths which, though rugged, have gripe in them, have in themselves presumptive evidence of their truth. We are to have toleration, but not of falsehood, nor that which is founded on indifference to the truth. It makes all the difference between life and death, between destruction and salvation, what a man believes. Because a man sincerely believes there is no chasm before him, when there *is* one there, will God the sooner save that man's neck if he goes forward?

Most of the religious controversies are of details. The great denominations now stand apart from each other on grounds which, by their own general confession, do not touch the individual Christian character.

If there was no grit in a grindstone, how long would the axe be in grinding? and if affairs had no pinch in them, when would there be made a man? How can a man walk by faith, unless compelled to go where he cannot see?

The most powerful way of teaching truth is to show what it has done for you.

Sentimental aspirations after goodness may be very well in their way; but it takes more than these to make a saint. A man (or a woman) may sit and read the Bible all day, and cry over it, and think how precious and holy it is, and how good God is, and then may go away and pray all night; but if the reading, and reflection, and praying, don't make a better man of him—if their effect is not to brighten and sweeten his disposition, and make him more kind and loving to God's creatures that are in his company, or in his power—if he can shut his Bible, and turn with scowling brow and unpitying heart to the orphan or the stranger within his gates, he has the very spirit of the Pharisee. He that loves God let him love his brother also.

God works by the church just as far as he can, but when she makes herself stiff or shallow, his workings overflow and run in a hundred ducts besides.

Those who think that the whole army of human deeds must go roaring through the thoroughfares of life whelming men in the general rush, and that no Sabbath notice must be taken of it—who make the pulpit too holy, and the Sabbath too sacred, to be used in bringing individual courses and developments of society to the bar of God's word for trial, are the lineal descendants of those Jews who considered the Sabbath so sacred that our Saviour desecrated it by healing the withered hand. Would God he could appear to his church in this our day and heal withered hearts.

THE world was made what it is that you might be made what you ought to be. Your daily duties are a part of your religious life just as much as your devotions are.

BECAUSE our impressions are right we have no business to flash them, unpreparedly and unadvisedly, in the faces of men.

THE test of a good institution is that it digs its own grave; for institutions are to humanity but what scaffolding is to a house, or a mould to the thing that is moulded.

WHEN God means to make a man useful in the world, he generally sends him first through fire—he puts him into the forge and onto the anvil—and often he chastens most whom he loves best.

Men confound earnestness and solemnity. A man may be very much in earnest and not be very solemn; or he may be awfully solemn without a particle of earnestness. A solemn nothing is just as wicked as a witty nothing. A man may be a repeater of stale truisms, he may smother living truths by conventional forms and phrases, but if he put on a very solemn face, and employ very solemn gestures before an audience of sound men—men soundly asleep, at least—that will pass for decorous handling of God's truth. The difference between Christ and his contemporary teachers was that he spoke live truths with the power of his own life in their utterance. The rabbins spoke old orthodoxy, dead as a mummy; but they spoke it very reverently; they never violated any professional propriety; they never forgot how to move, how to speak, how to maintain professional dignity. They forgot nothing except living truths and living souls. What if they did not do any good? What if everybody died about them? What if they never had any fruit? They charged that all to divine sovereignty.

Young Christians often get discouraged, and think that they bear no fruit, and shall be cut off. They see that Christ promised his disciples that he would dwell in them, and that they shall bear much fruit. Christ did not mean that fruit should come at once, all ripened. Remember to whom he spoke——men who were for years after this getting it through their heads that he was to die for them. It was twenty years before the fruit grew upon them that we find clustering in the epistles; and then only two or three of them had anything to do out of their own time.

When the gardener looks in the spring to see if the branches of his vines are alive, he is satisfied if he sees the tip of the most tiny bud—he don't call that a dead branch. There was but one of the disciples that seemed much changed for the better, during the life of Christ—that was John. He was one of those persons who, soft and velvety outside, have in them a core of granite, who, under a smooth aspect, carry the charge of thunder. He was the one who wanted to call down fire from heaven to burn up the people who had offended his Master. His affections, when not disturbed, were tender and sweet; but thwarted, he grew bitter as gall. Yet he came at last to that gentleness of character, by which he is now known; and, after a score of years, grew able to pen those fervent letters, so remarkable for ringing all the changes of love. Indeed John seems to have forgot every word in the language but "love." It is not in one year, nor five, nor ten, that you will ripen.

But you are dissatisfied, and you sit down and try to think how Christ looks, and try to feel that he is with you; and you take the Bible, expecting that now you are converted, it will shine out at you like a house whose windows are illuminated. Christ will not reveal himself to you in that way, and that is not the manner in which the Bible will be a light to you. You must make it "the man of your counsel." What a word is that! what an idea it gives you of how you should use the Bible.

A man offers you a note. You are not quite sure about it. You say to him: "I don't know. Hold on; I'll let you know in half an hour;" and away you run, round the corner. Your lawyer lives near by. You show him the note. "Such a one offered me this. I thought I'd just speak to you about it. What would you do?" "Better have nothing to do with it," says the lawyer, shaking his head. You run back, and say to the man: "I've concluded not to take that note."

Then some transaction is urged upon you. You hesitate. You don't know exactly whether it will stand in law: "Wait," you say, "wait a minute—I can't decide yet," and away you go, round the corner. "Oh, yes," says your lawyer, "that's all perfectly right and safe;" and back you run, and the matter is settled. He is the "man of your counsel." Just in this way should you consult the Bible, in regard to all the actions of your life. You may read all your life in it, and never get the meaning out of half its texts; for I think that many texts of Scripture are long in their periods, like comets, and only cast their light upon us when the appointed time comes; but unlike the comet, when once they have risen upon our horizon, they leave it no more, but their splendor burns on bright unto the end. There are texts which I got into twenty years ago, and I'm not half through them yet.

Christian graces are not in the Bible. The Bible tells us what they are; but it is in the struggle of life that we are to find them. A book of tactics is good to teach the soldier evolutions, but it is the parade ground and the battle-field that makes veterans. Men *can* make an idol of the Bible.

Each one of our faculties, when well cultivated, becomes an interpreter of God, a window through which we can look out and see God. Take benevolence; in its natural state 'tis mere good-nature, not much of a window then; but when you have exercised and trained it, until you see the interest of another lying side by side, on the same plane with yours, and can choose that first, doing good to another rather than to yourself; when you give up rest, and comfort, and health itself; when you uncomplainingly endure martyrdom and crucifixion for the sake of your nervous, and sick, and fretful children, who have wound you up, and run you down, and almost worn you out, *then* your benevolence shows you what kind of feeling was Christ's when he suffered and died for you.

It is all very well to have a minister to preach about religion; but you get used to him. I stand here, and say over and over to you the same things till I wear the year smooth. Every Christian who has come to a realization of Christ, is a natural and appointed preacher of him. You all know what is the effect here, when from one part of the room and another, men rise to corroborate each other's witness to the truth and effects of religion. Now, if the church would make the week a witness that should answer back and confirm the Sabbath; if you, in all your places of business, about the streets, everywhere, would but corroborate, by word and deed, in spirit and in truth, all the truths that I utter from the pulpit; if the young convert would call to the companions that he has left in the world, and the more advanced Christian would encourage the young one, and the white-haired saint again stand on the heights, and call: "Come up, come; from where we stand can be seen the gates of the Holy City," how would the influence of the church be felt, and how would be hastened the conversion of the world!

WHEN we begin to climb a hill, 'tis hard work; we begin to puff, our legs begin to ache, and by the time we reach the top of the hill, we are pretty well tired out. But once up, we begin to descend, and now we wonder that we could have made so much ado about our climbing. We resolve that we never will do so again. And we shall not until the next time. But when another hill is to be ascended, it will be the same thing over, unless we resolve with something more than the ordinary firmness of men.

There are hills in the moral as well as in the natural world, and we manage worse about the former than the latter.

How few people there are who have a really trusting spirit. 'Tis easy enough to trust, in regard to things you don't care anything about; but upon the point where you are most sensitive, how far do you trust in God, and not worry? Have you, within five years, learned to trust yourself and your property, and the health and life of those dearest to you, with God, in a settled confidence that he will do what is best with all? And can you be cheerful in this trust? The husbandman goes often to examine whether his fruit ripens fast. You are spiritual husbandmen, and should do likewise. It is astonishing, as one walks the streets, to see *how few good-looking people there are.* Very rare is it to see a luminous, transparent face, open and trustful. There are such natures, but they are rare. There are some people that can trust God about everything, but their soul's salvation.

When a hunter goes out to hunt, he seldom finds all that he hits. But going about the woods the next day, he finds here a buck, there a turkey, and something else elsewhere. "Ah!" he says, "I thought I brought down more game than I found yesterday. Here it is now." As I go about the country lecturing, I am so frequently being met by persons who say to me, shaking my hand: "I was converted among you. I have reason to know YOU, though you don't know ME," that I am beginning to feel that, on these jaunts, I only go a little wider into my own field of jurisdiction. Lately I was struck by the gratitude and humility of a mother whose son came last winter to New York. With parting injunctions and prayers, the mother very earnestly warned her boy to keep out of dangerous places; and, *especially* to be sure and not go near that wicked place, Henry Ward Beecher's church. She made this such a particular object of her caution, that, of course, the young man came. He was converted, and returned to his mother so changed, that she, too, was *converted.* When I was there, she, from gratitude, had gone over as far one way, as she had been the other; and was feeling very bad to think she had judged ill of one, who, since he was the instrument of her dear son's conversion, must be so very good a man. I do feel that the influence of this church is wide. There will hardly be, ere long, a town in the land that will not have branches from us. How humble and how careful ought they who exert so wide-spreading an influence to be.

When I dig a man out of trouble, the hole that he leaves behind him is the grave where I bury my own trouble.

There are some assertions of Scripture which imply high attainments in the whole round of

Christian character. "If any man offend not in word, the same is a perfect man;" that is, if a man has obtained that self-command which shall enable him never to say a wrong thing, the battle with him is nearly over. He may reckon it already won.

"God so loved the world that he gave his only begotten Son," etc. The life and death of Christ was but the working out of the love of God. The affection and the yearning of heart towards his erring creatures, was just the same in God before Christ came, that Christ showed it to be while he was on earth. It is just the same still. There is *no change* in God, or in his love. Man, nor woman, need fear disappointment *there*. It has been the custom of some, a custom too much prevailing, to represent God as being under no manner of obligation to do anything for his creatures after they had broken his law. The trouble with this statement is that there is a great deal of truth in it; and yet it has been made in such a manner as to give a very wrong impression. In God's own nature there is a *necessity* for his efforts for man's redemption. Where is the earthly father, worthy to bear the name, who would not feel that it was as much his duty as his desire to do all in his power to restore to the paths of honor and honesty a child who had fallen? And, shall we imagine that God, the Infinite Father, is under less obligations to do good to the creatures he has made than we are? or that the laws by which his nature are governed are directly the reverse of those which he has imprinted in our souls? "God is so great!" say some; and they hold up that greatness—sincerely desiring to show forth his praise, though mistaken in the thing wherein lies his greatest glory—not till they seat him on a throne *so* high that no man can touch even its base; till they cut him entirely off from man's sympathy. They say he might have justly let the world alone, after its revolt, and have concerned himself no more about it; and they declare the love and mercy which refused to do so, past finding out—a mystery of love at which mortals should forever wonder and adore. Yes, he might have let his rebels alone, in such a way that there would have been no propagation of the condemned and hopeless race; but that he did *not* do this, can any heart that is a parent's marvel? Man *can* understand God, when God has given, in his own breast, the key which can unlock his mysteries—*made in the image of God.*

God is great! but in proportion to his greatness is his love, and his obligation to do good. No being in the wide universe is so marked out and belted around with "ought"—with obligations to rectitude, as is the Almighty.

Because he is mighty and high is not the reason why he has a right to make conditions, and mark out the bounds of men—but because his wisdom and his goodness are so great. It is for *their own sake*, as well as for his, that God would have men serve him ; for all good and all happiness are inevitably connected with his service. This is in the nature of things. He loves every one of us with a warmer and heartier love than that which it is possible for the fondest of our human friends to feel for us ; and all his desires and all his commands are for our eternal good. His help is so often promised that men have got an idea that it is some nearly impossible thing one has to do in order to become a Christian ; but this is wrong. The help that we need is already with each one of us. In every man's hand God hath put a price with which to get wisdom, and if he does not obtain it, he will have none but himself to blame. We are asked to do nothing but what we can do, and do do every day, only not towards God. Who does not often feel the sense of guilt ? Who is there that has not often regretted a wrong act ? Who is there that has not faith in things unseen ? Who is there that has no power to love that which is lovely ?

My hearers, if it should be that any of you stand unfriended at the judgment, unclothed and shivering before the Judge, it will not be his voice alone that you will hear pronouncing sentence against you. Your own understanding, your own conscience and social affections, even your own worldly wisdom, will cry out that your ruin was needless, that it was only because you would not that you was not saved.

THE more refined and elevated men are, the more sensitive are they—the more is expected from them. A thing that you would pass without notice in a low, ignorant person, you would expect and demand apology for in a person higher on the social plane. Man, as well as God, exacts from man according to that which he hath.

THE present time with men, is as the sight of a rifle. They look through it to see what is before them.

CHANGES of motive and purpose are often instantaneous; but it may take years to get all the conduct in exact agreement with that changed mind. Suppose that the men on board a pirate vessel began to falter in their purpose, and to talk to each other about becoming honest seamen. By and by, having consulted all but the captain, they conclude to refer the whole matter to him; and if he consents they will all abandon the life of pirates.

They surround their captain, and make known to him their thoughts. "The whole thing depends on you, captain; what do you say?"

The captain thinks and thinks—he shakes his head. "I don't know, boys, about this. If we begin to be honest men, we must hold out so; and perhaps we can't. And then we may get caught and punished for what we *have* done. Still, I don't know. I guess we will give up this way of life—we —I suppose we *had* better decide to do so—we *will.*"

It was done—at that instant the men had ceased to be pirates. True, the black flag still swung from their mast; the last blood was hardly washed from their decks; they had been fitted out to attack and plunder the West Indian islands; and they were still full of the implements of death. But no matter, they were no longer pirates, any more than when they had pulled down the flag, cast away their weapons, and entered upon their lawful voyage.

The Lord's Prayer stops at "deliver us from evil." The doxology, though excellent, is generally admitted to be an interpolation. Who may pray? May the Christian? certainly. It has been considered that prayer was a privilege peculiarly that of the saint. This is an error. *Whoever has a want*, may pray. Has not the man in the fire or in the flood, a right to cry out for help, regardless of his character? What! may the *sinner* address God? Well, if "the sinner" may not, *who* in this wide world may? But "the sacrifice of the wicked is an abomination to the Lord," says Scripture. That passage has been wrested till it has been made the means of the loss of many souls; it has gone up and down the earth, destroying like a sword. It is the *hypocritical* sacrifice that God abhors. No *earnest* heart-sent cry is displeasing to him. When a man who would twist his neighbor's neck for gain, or who for it would thrust his arm up to the shoulder in blood, who loves and means to continue in the indulgence of riot, uncleanliness and wassail, makes his sacrifice, or offers his prayer for the sake of covering his real character; or, saying in his heart, "There! I hope that's enough to keep me safe"—*that* is the abomination of which the Bible speaks.

How should men pray? If any man can best approach God, and open his heart to him by means of prearranged prayers, in God's name, allow him to use them. But the spontaneous utterance of thought, feeling and desire is best suited for specific cases. Printed prayers are generic.

By his conduct and his relations, Christ taught

that it was God's pleasure to be *taken firm hold of* by the soul in prayer. He taught us plainly that there are some things which he will give to his children if they will plead for them long enough, and with sufficient intensity of desire, and which *otherwise* they shall not have. He enjoined it upon us that in prayer we should be, to *the last degree*, earnest, constant, and importunate. But God wants no man to make watch-preparation for communion with him. Don't look at your watch, and say, "It's noon, or it's six o'clock—I must go and pray—whether you've anything to say or not. Some men pray three times a day; they have three regular hours. If this suits their case let them do it. Others pray regular oral prayers but once a day. There are some birds that sing when the sun rises, and then they are done for that day. All Christians ought to be much in prayer. They should even in secret pray with the voice—for the voice helps to fix the thoughts; and no man will ever grow much in the grace of praying who prays in his heart *only*. Social prayer also is a duty and a benefit to the Christian; but, above all things, let them strive to be sincere, simple, and natural in prayer. Faults of manner in addressing God are not confined to young converts—if so, there would be more prospect of having them all corrected. The young should beware of falling into these faults. Don't allow yourself to have a praying tone, one much higher or lower than that which is natural to you. The moment I hear a man go up or down an octave in his voice, I am left an octave behind. Then some men's voices have a roll, they have a swinging undulation like the waves of the sea. All this is very unpleasant —even revolting to refined taste.

When young Christians complain to me that their thoughts wander in their devotions, I tell them that they pray too much. Pray often, *but not* too long at a time. I have heard very stammering, staggering prayers—prayers that broke down in the middle, that were yet real, living prayers. Far better are such than those whose composition is perfect, but in which words have outrun feeling. All the first troubles in regard to this intercourse and confidence with God will pass, and, by and by, the Christian who really desires it, will come to live, as it were, in a perpetual prayer. He will walk through the days with a consciousness that he *is* "naked and open before him with whom he has to do," and he will rejoice in that consciousness. Every new event, every new emotion of his life will be with him an impulse towards God. He must tell it there. His confidences and his warmest gushes of feeling are continually lifting themselves up to the being of his supreme love and reverence; and *this* is to "pray without ceasing." When the heart of man attains unto this state, he can no more be left comfortless or alone, though the grave hide all who love him, and though a dungeon shut him from the light of day.

You will frequently need some preparation for prayer. When a man is full of the fretting cares of business; sore, smarting, tormented by the untoward events of the day, he often feels that he is in an unfit state to enjoy communion with his Maker. The mind needs some relief before it can settle itself to prayer. With me music is one of the best aids here. One deep and solemn strain of music is enough to separate as far between me and any past state of mind, as the Red Sea separated between Pharaoh and the Israelites.

---

*O, GOD! we know not what life in heaven is; nor what disposition is made of occupation there; but we know that whatever *here* is most bright, whatever is most beautiful and lovely, whatever is most delightful in experience and most pleasing in sensation, is used to excite our imagination of the joys that await thy children, and that after all these things are exhausted we are told that it doth not *yet* appear what we shall be.

* The following passages are from prayers by Mr. Beecher.

How long, O, Lord! how long? Since thou wentest up into heaven, hast thou forgotten the earth?

Givest thou no more heed to the voice of her groaning?

For eighteen hundred years, since thy departure, she has swung round about thy throne, uttering, evermore her cries of bitterness and pain. Is it not enough? Oh! hear the wail of nature, and come, Lord Jesus, come *quickly*.

Thy coming, and that alone, can redeem us. And when thou art here, the waters of bitterness will all be turned to sweetness; and the song of earth, as she swings in her orbit, shall be like the melody of heaven.

Our Father, we love thee, though we so often grieve thee. Our God, our Saviour, we desire to walk in thy love; why *do* our feet so constantly falter?

Oh! come unto us, and possess us in every faculty of our souls. *Abide* with us, thou Heavenly Guest, and so draw us that we turn from thee no more.

When we look abroad into the world, and see what a place it is; see how full it is of jangling and selfishness; of violence, of passion and blood; thy Fatherhood, and our brotherhood unacknowledged, and men everywhere at strife. And when we look *within*, and see the evil there: the lurking enemies, crouching in secret places, waiting for us to lie down in slumber, or to ungird our armor for a moment's rest, that they may spring out and assassinate us, we are ready to sink down in despair, and cry out that all is lost, and that thou hast indeed forsaken us. But we know that thou art not gone—that thou art *not* afar off, and that thou dost regard the cry of thy children.

Then, hear us now, O, God! while we reach out after thee, and are sick for want of thee. Come unto us with healing, and speak comfortable things unto us, and hasten the salvation of the world.

When the clouds are over us so black that those who know thee not, see in them only wrath and destruction, may we, looking up, behold and know that thou art near, and that we are only standing in the twilight of the shadow of our God.

May we be over-arched by our faith in Thee; may we stand under it as our shadow and protection from all the storms, and sins, and woes of life.

While we walk through the places of crucifixion here, may the thought of our Father's home sustain us.

Is our home indeed awaiting us? *Art* thou looking upon us with yearning, and thinking that the time draws near when thou mayest call us to thine arms? *Dost* thou love us, and long for us, oh! our God? for *us*, so full of all unquietness and uncleanness, so barren of all loveliness.

"Oh! teach us the meaning of that word "Love." Teach us, too, that with thee it means not less, but more than it does in the truest and warmest human heart—that our love is as the brook, shallow and defiled, while thine is as the ocean flowing to meet the brook, and swallowing up all its impurity as though it had not been.

May the thought of thy tenderness and pity give us courage. May it not encourage us to think sin less dreadful, but cause us to hate and shun it more; and yet, in spite of all our oft falling and failing, to take comfort in thee; and to struggle, not from fear, and to escape thy frown, but with a great yearning to get upward nearer and nearer to thy smile.

May the thought of thy love make sin more hateful and fearful to us than all the thunderings of conscience ever did; and may it look even blacker while we feel the throbbings of thy divine pity, than when viewed in the light of thy pure and perfect law.

Our Father, may grieving thee be the one

terror of our lives. Teach us *how* to love each other, and how, hating all sin, to have mercy on the sinner, even as thou dost. Look not upon our sins, nor enter into judgment against us, for which of us could stand one moment before thee?

WHEN we are alone and desolate—forsaken of all that makes life dear, be not thou afar off. Be near us, O Thou who canst make thyself so much more unto us than parents, or brother, or sister, or husband, or wife, or lover, or friend: for these are but sparks struck out from thee. They are only names, which, gathered and grouped together, mean God.

To trust in human love is often to be pierced as with thorns; to lean on human faithfulness is to feel the broken shaft enter our side; but no man ever trusted in Thy love and found it grow cold towards him; no heart ever yearned towards Thee, and stayed itself upon Thee, and found Thee unfaithful or unkind.

WE pray Thee that Thou wilt give us grace to bear with the troubles that are in our daily life. What are we that we should ask to go crowned with joy when all through the world there is so much sorrow? We pray thee not so much to take away our burdens, not so much to lift from us the cross, or to pluck away the thorns, as to show us how patiently and lovingly to bear them.

Our days are passing; O God! that dwellest where they sing who have done with weeping; they whom we buried with tears and anguish, but whom thou didst raise again with gladness and everlasting exaltation; and hast given them so much more and better than we, in our largest and most ardent desires, know how to ask for them, that they, looking down from their glorious exaltation, see immeasurably below them the *dust* that we have named as blessings; when it shall be our turn to hear that call which men name "death," may we, waking as children called by mother's voice at morning, see bending above us thy face of eternal beauty and infinite love, and feel beneath us thine everlasting arms, and break into the first notes of that rapturous song which shall not cease, with our head upon thy bosom.

Be with and bless our friends, wherever they are. Scattered abroad in the earth, they are toiling, each with his duties and his burdens, and his wearing sorrows. *We* would fain gather them in the bosom of our love, O Lord! and there shelter and give them consolation; but it cannot be; for our hearts are filled with their own burdens and sorrows, and they are powerless to bear even these alone—how then shall we help our brothers; but what is *our* love and pity when compared with thine? And, are they not all beneath the shadow; nay, in the sunshine of thy care? and canst thou, without whom not a sparrow's strength faileth, permit any heart that stays itself on thee to be broken by its trouble? Thou wilt *never* leave us nor forsake us; and they that are ours by love are parts of our own soul, and the promise and the covenant is for them also. Therefore, O our God! we commit those united to us, yet, by space, divided from us, into thy faithful and tender keeping, and we *know* that they are safe.

OUR* souls rejoice, O Thou blessed one! when we feel ourselves drawn towards Thee, for it is not in *us* to rise; and when our thoughts are all tending with sweet affection towards heaven, we know that there have been solicitations, and that God hath yearned for us, and hath sent forth ministering influences to waken love, and lift our souls towards him. And as the sun doth draw up all vapors, and wreathe the mountain tops therewith, so in Thy

* A Prayer from a Phonographic Report in the American Pulpit, by Prof. Henry Fowler.

high and holy place—yea, towards Mount Zion above, Thou, with sweet and blessed looking, dost draw our affections; and our hearts to-day exhale towards Thee.

For though we have not seen Thee, we *know* Thee, Thou mighty one! Though we have never beheld Thee in outward form and guise, our hearts have taken hold upon Thee.

The hand that was pierced for us hath never been laid upon us in our path; nor have those sacred wounded feet crossed our threshold; but that heart, that mind of Thine, the *soul of God*, hath crossed the threshold of our dwellings; and with our hearts, full often, we have had communion with Thee, as friend with friend.

And in the times of darkness, and of temptation, we have wrestled with Thee, even as the Patriarch of old, and thou hast given us victories, which the tongue may not mention, but which the heart will think of with joy and everlasting gratitude.

In times when affliction seemed to dissolve us—when our heart was as fruit about to drop from the bough, when there was no more strength by which to lay hold upon life, thou hast come, Thou blessed one! and given us strength again to lay hold on life, and to be happy in life, and to rise above the darkness of personal distress, and the struggle and the conflict of immingled evils. We have been fearful of dangers; but afterwards Thou hast made us to laugh, as children laugh when alarmed and then looking back, see that it was but the shaking of a leaf. And when things have seemed to settle around us in darkness, and troubles have come thick upon us, Thou hast lifted us up, and put our feet upon a rock, where no tide could reach us and no wave could dash against us, and no flood could sweep with destroying eddies about us, to unsettle our peace, or do us harm in thought or feeling.

And we have been made masters that before were servants to our circumstances. We have been able to stand undaunted and to beat back troubles that came upon us. Thou hast lifted us up from sorrows, from violence, from unexpected evil. When periods of dismay have come drifting in upon us like diffused mist, cold and chill—those days of doubt when we could see nothing, when the pall of silence lay upon everything, then, likewise, Thou hast manifested thyself unto us. Thou hast given us, at last, a sweet patience to stand still, *and to wait;* and we have found that waiting by thy side is better than running alone; and that to be empty and weak, for Christ's sake, is better than to be full for our own sake.

We rejoice that Thou hast, in a thousand ways, manifested thyself to us in all the desires and yearnings of our hearts. We have looked out upon life sometimes with joy, and then with a sweet sadness, because, after all, there was so little in it that its brightness grew dim almost before it flashed its brightness forth; and we have been glad of it.

We thank Thee that Thou hast addressed thyself to us by our nobler thoughts, and redeemed the world from emptiness and given it back to us when we have yielded it to Thee, crowned and glorified. Thou hast made the things that are round about us—the very flowers that perish—the leaves that wither and drop away, the changes of the season—to be the teachers and Thy preachers to our souls.

But these things alone do not content us; for they are things of the lower life, and we have yearned for that which we have not. We have had divine incitements; we have had blessed inspirations; when all that we knew seemed so fragmentary, and all that we *were* so exceedingly little and less than fragmentary; when we have felt that our affections were so cold and ignoble; when from a thought of our own ungratefulness and selfishness and pride, we have turned to the bright vision of thy love—so sweet, so lasting, so deep, so gentle, so delicate beyond all expression from human tongue; when we have seemed to ourselves to be so coarse, so low, so ignoble, that we scarcely could lift up our eyes unto Thee. But Thou, O blessed one! hast been pleased to look upon us out of the brightness and radiance of thine own perfections. Out of the depth and purity and sweetness of Thine own love, Thou hast looked forgivingly upon our rudeness, and our hollowness, our pride, our selfishness, our jealousy; and hast uttered to our souls promises that we should not always be thus —that *if we would have faith Thou wouldst have patience;* and that Thou wouldst bring us onward and upward, step by step, shining brighter and brighter unto the perfect day.

Lord Jesus, Thou wilt not forsake one word Thou hast ever uttered. Thou wilt not betray one single hope or expectation in our hearts which Thou hast ever suggested; and all which Thou hast promised Thou wilt not only do, but exceeding abundantly more. Thou wilt outrun our most fruitful conceptions; Thou wilt be more gentle than our heart has felt in its most raptured moments; Thou wilt be more patient than our utmost conceptions of patience; Thou wilt be more full of love and goodness than our loftiest aspirations.

We rejoice that there is in Thee such infinite goodness, and such height, and length, and breadth, and depth of mercy.

Still, we are not *willing* to be sinful, or low, or ignorant, or poor, because of Thy goodness; though we have a strange wonder of gladness that we are weak, because it sets forth to us such glories in Thee, thou nourishing God! patient with us, as a nurse is patient with her children!

Yea! Thou hast thyself declared that the mother shall forget her nursing child sooner than Thou wilt forget those whom Thou dost love. We take the promise that is in Thy declarations and we set it against the darkness of time and trouble, and weighing down of heart with sadness, and we lift ourselves by this divine help above them all. When we stand under the darkest cloud, we see the bow of promise, and we know that God will not suffer the soul that loves him to be overwhelmed by any deluge.

And now may we have these bright days more frequently, so that their shining may cast a twilight into the dark days that intervene. As they that watch in the night shall behold the glowing light of morning reaching up the hillsides, mounting the highest cliffs, and coming down into the valleys beyond, so mayest thou who watchest for us, see that the light of hope and the glory of God is more and more perfectly enwrapping our whole experience. For it is Thy work, blessed Saviour; we are being fashioned by Thy hand, and for thy sake, as well as for our own. Thou art yet to present us spotless before the throne of Thy

Father, and heaven is to resound with acclamations for our sake, and for Thy sake.

Thou, Lord Jesus! thou who art mighty over all things, and with whom we are fellow-heirs, we rejoice that in all the things that we ask for ourselves there is also thine own interest, and thine own glory and joy enwrapped!

Now, we beseech of Thee that Thou wilt speak peaceably unto every heart in Thy presence this morning, according to our various necessity. If there be those here that do not know their own trouble, but only know that they *are* troubled—*Thou knowest*, and thou canst enter in, and make the darkest chamber of their heart serene with light and peace. We beseech of Thee that thou wilt sustain those who are bearing the pressure of affliction. Thou thyself didst bear affliction for them. Thou wert *acquainted* with grief. And may they look up, while their tears flow, into the face of Him who wept, who lived, who suffered, who died for them and for their consolation.

Grant Thy blessings to those who are suffering the bafflings and trials of poverty. Lord, are they poorer than thou wert, who hadst not where to lay thy head? Yet, so far as is consistent with their good, alleviate their trouble; raise them up friends and comforts of life.

Bless all those that are tried in their worldly

affairs; who, whatever way they turn, find fears prevailing. Will the Lord be gracious unto them that they may not think their life consisteth in the abundance of the things which they possess. May they feel that the things of this life and all the troubles that harass it pass quickly away; and may they also feel that they are not in any wise ruined, or overturned. May they lay up their treasures where no misfortunes may ever assail. May they believe in Him who is rich beyond all bankruptcy. We beseech of thee that thou wilt be very near to all that are in doubt of mind, and are perplexed in their thoughts and belief of things religious. Do Thou teach them the greatest of all truth—how *to love God*, and how to diffuse that love upon men. And may they, at last, find encouragement in this, that Thou art their God.

We beseech of Thee, that to all those who are in the trust of this life's prosperities, who are surrounded with friends and comforts, and who have been blessed abundantly, Thou wilt grant humility, that they may not become proud, nor hard and unfeeling towards those who are less successful and skillful than they; and by so much as they are above them, may they see to it not only that they use their goods, but also their hearts and minds for the benefit of their fellow-men.

Be near to strangers in our midst, whose hearts

yearn for those who have been wont to worship with them. Will the Lord bring them by faith very near. And as they meet at the foot of the cross, may they consciously be united to all who love the Lord Jesus, and whom they love.

Diffuse the blessings of the Gospel over all the earth. May slavery cease; may war cease; may intemperance cease; may justice reign, and *love* upon justice; and may the whole earth be filled with the glory of God! We ask it for Christ's sake. Amen.

www.ingramcontent.com/pod-product-compliance
Lightning Source LLC
LaVergne TN
LVHW020218110826
845151LV00003B/756

* 9 7 8 1 4 2 5 5 3 3 0 6 9 *